Forty Years in the Wilderness

Books by James W. Hulse

The Forming of the Communist International
Stanford University Press, 1964

The Nevada Adventure: A History
University of Nevada Press, 1965; 5th ed. 1981

Revolutionists in London:
A Study of Five Unorthodox Socialists
Oxford University Press, 1970

The University of Nevada: A Centennial History
University of Nevada Press, 1974

Forty Years in the Wilderness:
Impressions of Nevada, 1940–1980
University of Nevada Press, 1986

Forty Years in the Wilderness

IMPRESSIONS OF NEVADA 1940-1980

James W. Hulse

University of Nevada Press
Reno, Nevada
1986

NEVADA STUDIES IN HISTORY AND POLITICAL SCIENCE NO. 22

STUDIES EDITOR
Wilbur S. Shepperson

EDITORIAL COMMITTEE

Don W. Driggs   Joseph A. Fry
Jerome E. Edwards   Andrew C. Tuttle

Library of Congress Cataloging-in-Publication Data

Hulse, James W.
  Forty years in the wilderness.

(Nevada studies in history and political science; no. 22)
  Bibliography: p.
  Includes index.
  1. Nevada—History. I. Title. II. Series.
F841.H75   1986   979.3'033   85–24635
ISBN 0–87417–099–0

University of Nevada Press, Reno, Nevada 89557 USA
© James W. Hulse 1986. All rights reserved
Cover design by Dave Comstock
Printed in the United States of America

CONTENTS

Foreword   ix
Preface   xv

1. The State, the Towns, and the People: 1940   1
2. The Four Nevadas Revisited: 1980   11
3. The Struggles for Water   29
4. The Land and Its Uses   47
5. The Utopia for Gamblers   65
6. Beyond the Glitter: A State Without a Conscience   87
7. A Fifth Nevada: With a Conscience?   113

Notes   123
Bibliography   131
Index   137

And so, in such a wilderness, the tempo is—always has been—that each man should be capable of looking out for himself. If he is not capable, he can get out, he can go "over the hill," meaning over the Sierra to California. If he wants to gamble, the prerogative is his own. But he must not hang around whining if he loses, nor ask the state for recompense, nor for a free living ever afterwards.

Max Miller, *Reno* (1941)

And so goes the dismal story of Nevada's niggardliness. Too rich to accept normal taxes, too poor to maintain its institutions and agencies on a decent twentieth-century level, coddling known racketeers and making them respectable by legalizing their operations, while turning a cold poormaster's eye to its poor, its sick, its socially misshapen . . .

There are, of course, many good people in Nevada, concerned about the deplorable neglect of child and adult unfortunates, and wanting to do something about it. But they don't set the effective health and welfare policies of the gambling state, nor have they been able to modify it much—as yet. An awakened citizenry will someday take into account the human costs of a gambling economy, and act on it, building up the vast potentials of this fabulously beautiful state.

Albert Deutsch, "The Sorry
State of Nevada," *Collier's* (1955)

FOREWORD

THE FOLLOWING STUDY of contemporary Nevada society is unique in that it is a thoughtful questioning of the state's key source of revenue, gambling. One reader summarized the thrust of the manuscript in a single sentence. "If Nevada's institutions are to be salvaged from the voraciousness of the dominant industry [gambling] a guilt complex must be cultivated, a spirit of atonement fostered." Indeed, the author of *Forty Years in the Wilderness* calls for a five-year moratorium on casino expansion and an orderly build-down in all gambling operations. He argues that as gaming interests have gained greater economic dominance and political influence within the state we, the citizens, have tended to ignore their "sintality," that is, the negative impact that gambling has come to have upon the amorphous mass of all society. The author suggests that the basic criterion to be used in measuring the true value of the institution is to evaluate its contributions to social legislation, education, artistic endeavor, cultural progress, in short, to investigate the industry's stimulation of the whole fabric of community life.

The previous twenty-one publications presented in the History and Political Science Series have varied considerably in both format and content, and a few have stimulated mild academic controversy. The present study is more complex, however, in that it deals with a society's sensibilities. Depending on the reader's point of view, this book might be classified as a journalistic essay, a historical survey, a personal memoir, or a moral admonition. The Polish American poet and Nobel

Prize winner Czeslaw Milosz argues that "a writer can afford to produce in his lifetime one maverick work." Certainly James Hulse has earned his spurs as a student of both local history and world politics. He has written on the Greeks, the Soviet Union, and the *Revolutionists in London*. As background for *Forty Years in the Wilderness,* he has authored a textbook on the state, a centennial history of the University of Nevada, and a study of his home region, Lincoln County.

As in most maverick works, Hulse allows many self-portraitures to slip through. As a native, he is mesmerized by the spectacular force of Nevada's mountains and deserts. While he has achieved a fairly comfortable academic preferment, the state's current cultural outlook has come to embarrass and worry him. He borrows from Henry Adams in calling himself a "conservative Christian anarchist" who is alternately filled with feelings of anger, despair, and hope. He has not been able to distance himself from Nevada reality by spinning a cocoon in the state university or even through lengthy residencies in France, Switzerland, and England. Hulse knows that the anti-ideological character of the state has something to do with our much-touted easygoing relationships and that the study of Nevada's peculiar institutions is in a very real sense a study of ourselves. These institutions are the early child of the American West, and we have been their architect as well as the eager recipients of the wealth they accrue.

Obviously the benevolent attitude of Nevadans toward gambling and the get-rich-quick syndrome is not new. The early settlers of the West showed little social responsibility as they eliminated Indians, eagerly dug for precious ore, built livestock empires, appropriated the small streams of fresh water, cut forests, and ignored both the needs of their neighbors and of the future while destroying the environment. In Nevada, divorce, prostitution, gambling, boxing, and other "sports" were legitimized for quick and easy profit. Maybe citizens are the culprits as well as the victims. Maybe the enemy is to be seen in the mirror as well as in "glitter gulch."

About two years ago when I first discussed the present essay with the author, I questioned if he could pull together the many threads of contemporary Nevada life into a single illuminating tapestry. He has, but not all will agree with the conclusions. Indeed, the very purpose and design of the work make it likely that every serious reader will find statements with which to differ. For example, the suggestion that traditional rural Nevada is morally more exacting than the growing urban centers is perhaps an attractive myth. Almost two hundred years ago, Jane Austen declared, "The most unscrupulous activities need a rural atmosphere in which to flourish." Furthermore, most of the world's great concepts were born in brash, overcrowded urban centers like Jerusalem, Rome, Paris, and New York. And many contemporary pundits have suggested that the studios of Hollywood and the casinos of Las Vegas are creating new art forms and shaping new cultural dimensions.

In the first four chapters, Hulse evaluates the state's limited resources, migratory patterns, unstable population, and the uneven regional growth. Images and attitudes, ideas and interpretations, are woven into the irregular Nevada tapestry. In the last three chapters the gambling enterprise, as well as the criminal element it so often embraces, is pictured as a leviathan worthy of excoriation. Because of the multiple threads, scholarly reviewers have not been of one mind in their reaction to the manuscript. They have seen it as "a polemic," as "a reformist tract," as "a profound interpretation," and as "an Alice in Wonderland" scenario. Local citizens sensing little wrong with the state will be disturbed. Conversely, those who see Nevada as the Mafia's "great rotten borough" will find the work devoid of easy gossip. Some who argue that a professor of history should eschew judgment and deal only with documents and source material will be exasperated. But for those who seek Nevada's contemporary human biography, who wish to follow the unlikely parabola of its successes and failures, and who sense the love and anguish of one of its native sons, *Forty Years in the Wilderness* sounds a drumbeat of prophetic concern.

Perhaps it is Hulse's Mormon antecedents who brought him to crave greater ethical exactness, or perhaps it is his affinity for the ideas of nineteenth-century Unitarian teachers that led him to speak out, or perhaps it is his study of utopian radicals that caused him to appreciate the thinking of visionaries and rebels. Whatever the reason, Hulse is deeply disturbed by the state's problems and shortcomings and has come to believe that those with knowledge and missionary zeal must put things right. He would argue that you *can* go home again. By diagnosing our cultural failures and prescribing cures for our many ills, he is following a long-standing tradition among American writers. He accepts the progressive approach to history with its evolutionary view of social progress and successive achievements. But he does more than diagnose and accept—he demands action, he is not the plaintive passive professor. He follows in the footsteps of his mentor, the author and teacher Charlton Laird, who once defined a professor as one who "works as much by difference as by community, and more by dissent than by acceptance, although he must want to accept. . . . He wants to believe in mankind, and mostly he can."

Although a historian, Hulse is not writing *Forty Years* as a man of memory or as a man of the past. Rather, he is writing very much as a contemporary and as a man preaching a transformation. He cautiously admires the old rough and masculine frontier, but, like Emerson in the essay on *Power,* Hulse thinks it is time to pass from the "savage with all his hairy Pelasgic strength" to a "new sense of beauty." Like Emerson, Hulse wants the "swarthy juices . . . to flow plentifully . . . but their astringency or acridity is got out by ethics and humanity." In brief, he wants Nevada to prosper but with culture and morality as major objectives. Like the early Unitarians who were also tied to the growing wealth of the industrial revolution, Hulse embraces the motto "The good life is more than material decency."

In all of this Hulse reflects a basic, indeed a classical, American mystique. Careful European observers of American life, like Michael Howard, Regius Professor of Modern History at Oxford, suggest that we find a common identity not in ethnic community or shared historical experiences but rather in a value system and that our basic cohesion, or lack of it, is based upon a reiteration of these values. While Europeans readily understand strategic, economic, political, and even cultural arguments, they are uniformly confused by our emphasis on morals, ethics, and humanity. Recently the Kissinger Commission on Central America declared our first interest was to "preserve the moral authority of the United States" and "to be perceived by others as a nation that does what is right because it is right." Just as America has always produced the hustlers, the snake oil salesmen, and the Babbitts, we have also been a land of reformers, muckrakers, and prohibitionists. We never cease to embrace the new crusade, the square deal, the fair deal, the new patriotism, or the moral majority. Therefore *Forty Years* is vintage Americana. It is designed to address our internal conflict, to restore our true moral autonomy and to give us back to ourselves.

Publishers and editors must ask of any prospective book: What are the author's motives for writing and who is the audience? Neither fiction nor a textbook, *Forty Years* was not written to make money. Nor is the overriding purpose to explore an audience or to respond to the challenge of colleagues or even to reveal a truth. *Forty Years* is designed to appeal to the good sense and nobility of all citizens. There are no disguises, subterfuges, or anonymities; there are no equivocations, perplexing ironies, or complex ambiguities. When the work upbraids and goads

Nevadans for their many ethical and cultural failures, the author is speaking from that lonely height where the artist and the crusader, not the historian or politician, is hero.

But, conversely, Hulse is also writing to say thank you, to render gratitude to the state he so intimately loves, and perhaps to try again to sever his own umbilical cord. Part of his energy for the project comes from a wish to reciprocate. As one who has spent thousands of hours traversing the landscape, fishing the streams, chatting with old-timers, digging for ore, and reporting for local newspapers, he is both the product and the gadfly of his society. He is in the fortunate position of being able to express his feelings with his pen. James Hulse is a moralist like Isaiah, who, after richly condemning the waywardness and the falling away from the law of his beloved desert people, concluded by prophesying that with the restoration of perfection "every valley shall be lifted up and every mountain and hill be made low" and "then justice will dwell in the wilderness."

Wilbur S. Shepperson
January, 1985

PREFACE

SOME TIME AGO, the urge to clean out my Nevada files came over me once again. This time it was induced not by any sudden, temporary instinct for neatness or by a sentimental desire to reminisce. Too many years as an unreformed pack rat had finally caught up with me. So I began to cull and discard. The present volume is a condensation of some of that debris.

The forty-odd years under consideration coincide more or less with my own time of observation in Nevada. Many of the "impressions" assembled here are taken from the books or articles of informed outsiders, some from my fellow Nevadans. Initially I regarded this monograph as a kind of montage of such impressions, but the more I shoveled through my litter, the more clear it became that this work—even more than most—must stand or fall as a personal testimonial. I will not call it a work of history, although it necessarily bears the stamp of my professional orientation. It is essentially a social and political statement, based on some widely available technical, historical, and political documents and arranged in an idiosyncratic manner.

There are not many of us around who have lived in Nevada for most of the period between the 1930s and 1980s and who have had employment that has encouraged us to keep a running account of the main events in our bizarre commonwealth. It occurred to me, as I worked through my files, that I might be in a special position to offer some interpretations on the basis of my childhood in Pioche during the Depression and the Big

War, my years as a college student and newspaper reporter in Reno in the 1940s and 1950s, and my station in the battered little ivory tower that Nevadans have long called their university.

A description of assignments that have come my way over the years is not worthy of the readers' time here; this piece is not meant to be either a declaration of candidacy or an obituary. But it has been my fate to report on most state institutions at one time or another, to be involved in civil rights movements and partisan politics, to do historical-legal research on water and land problems, to joust in various academic tournaments, to know several generations of Nevada students, and to enjoy many friendships.

It would require a volume much larger than this one to acknowledge those who have had a part in this work. Those who have most often encouraged, criticized, and tolerated my thoughts on these matters are my former professors and and longtime colleagues Russell Elliott and Wilbur Shepperson. Jerome Edwards has also been most generous with his time and information. Several others who read or heard all or parts of it made useful comments. The staff of the University of Nevada Press has been most helpful and constructively critical. Agnes Cottino and William Metz have provided indispensable assistance as proofreader and critic. Many who read this document did not like it or objected to my conclusions, but all their objections were productive, and the work is less flawed than it would have been without their advice. Evelyne Wash has produced the maps for this volume in a most efficient and professional manner.

Several who looked at various drafts advised me to make it either more personal or less personal. It has not been possible to follow the advice of both camps, so I have persisted in my idiosyncratic methods. We never did build our reputations on conformity here in the Great Basin country.

Nevadans are jealous of their freedoms and privileges. They have often asserted that they have the right to set their land, water, gambling, and social policies without regard to the rest of the country. Perhaps it is time to reflect on the long-term consequences of this attitude and to conduct a dialogue on the question of whether the so-called liberal attitude toward gambling and other socially questionable activities, in combination with the distinctly stingy attitudes toward our social institutions, is the appropriate course for the years that may lie ahead of us.

CHAPTER 1

THE STATE, THE TOWNS, AND THE PEOPLE: 1940

SOME FORTY-FIVE years ago, shortly before the United States entered the Second World War, Nevada sat, in a manner of speaking, for a series of portraits. This most maligned and misunderstood of states, the ugly duckling of the federal American family, was paid the compliment of being sketched by a number of talented popularizing writers. Not since the days when Mark Twain and Dan De Quille described the Virginia City mining boom had there been such an array of social and literary practitioners to render its features in print. In retrospect, it appears that the fates, the government bureaus, and various penmen and penwomen conspired to etch the features of the commonwealth for posterity in about 1940–1941, before some of its rustic frontier features disappeared from view.[1]

Because of this coincidence that imprinted many data in a short period of time, we have a mosaic of social information that may be regarded, four decades later, as a starting point from which to measure the state's social trajectory toward the 1980s. The following pages try to chart that course, building on the data of the 1940s and extending them to the present decade.

Nevada's social history falls neatly into three forty-year periods. From 1859 until 1899, the state's residents witnessed the rise and fall of the silver mining towns, the most famous of which was Virginia City—the site of the famous Comstock Lode and the Big Bonanza. A dozen other mining camps enjoyed shorter periods of prosperity, but all ultimately suffered the humiliating experience of "borrasca," which a rhetorically imaginative journalist defined as "out of ore and out of luck." For the last twenty years of the nineteenth century, Nevada languished economically, its population fell to 40,000, and eastern critics occasionally asked whether such a thinly populated and socially retarded cluster of desert outposts was worthy of the status of statehood within the federal Union.

Beginning in 1900, the second forty-year period opened with the discovery of new ore bodies in the south-central part of the state. The silver veins of Tonopah, the rich specimens of the "yellow metal" at Goldfield, and the huge copper deposits near Ely initiated the "twentieth-century mining boom," as Russell Elliott appropriately called this revival. Like the first boom, it lasted for about twenty years, stimulated prospecting in many parts of the state and the building of a number of new railroads, and then—like the first boom—ended in depression and frustration.[2]

Then in about 1940, just as the Second World War brought a bonanza of new defense-related and military activities to the Southwest, Nevadans began to discover ways to profit from one of the quaint social notions that they had retained from bonanza days—the permissive view of gambling. With a casual attitude that might be described as social absentmindedness, the state made gambling its pivotal business. Gradually, without much attention to the consequences, it devised a strategy for channeling tens of thousands, then millions, then hundreds of millions of dollars through the casinos with the help of some of the nation's most notorious racketeers. It has been slow to evaluate the consequences for its own citizenry and American society as a whole.

The Accidental State

The Nevada of 1940 was both the victim and the beneficiary of its peculiar geography and history. Nature, so generous in its gifts to other parts of the North American continent to the east and west, denied this region nearly all of the assets that had made America so attractive to the immigrants of European descent. It was and is one of the most arid parts of the country. Its rigorous high-desert climate forced the aboriginal Americans who lived upon it to scratch desperately and wander widely to find their game, grasses, insects, and pinion nuts for sustenance. It was the last part of the United States to be thoroughly explored. The first men of European descent to see it, the trappers with Peter Skene Ogden and Jedediah Smith in 1826 and 1827, passed through it as quickly as they could, finding few fur-bearing animals or other articles of value. Only in the 1840s, when the emigrant trains began their treks to California and explorers like John Frémont undertook systematic surveys of the Far West, did the essential features of the vast Great Basin and upper Mohave Desert become known. Then there followed swiftly the conquest of the entire Southwest by the Americans in the Mexican War of 1846–1848, the incursion of the Mormons into the valley of the Great Salt Lake in 1847, and the Gold Rush to California in 1849–1850.

In the 1850s, the western Great Basin was a thoroughfare, but it was not yet a distinct social entity in any minds or on any maps. At the midpoint of the nineteenth century, the happenstances of history began to plant and nourish the seeds of a new state in that wilderness, even though it was a poor soil for such an undertaking. When the people who founded California were sitting in their constitutional convention in Monterey in 1849, they confronted the question of where they should place the eastern boundary of their new commonwealth. They considered, among other possibilities, both the crest of the Sierra Nevada and the summits of the Rocky Mountains. There was no compelling reason for them to select, as they did, the 120th meridian west of Greenwich. They knew only vaguely where that artificial line was, and only many years later was there a definitive survey. Had they chanced to place their boundary one degree further east, Congress would probably have endorsed it. In that case, the attractive valleys east of the Sierra where Nevada was born and the vast treasures of the Comstock Lode would have been within California.[3]

Some Mormon traders established the first station in Carson Valley east of the Sierra in 1851, and at about the same time the first traces of gold appeared in the pan of a California-bound prospector. Within nine years, other miners had found the massive gold and silver deposits of the Comstock Lode, just as the Union began tearing itself apart in the Civil War. Shortly before Abraham Lincoln became president, Congress recognized the economic importance of the new discovery by creating the Territory of Nevada, and Lincoln was able to pay some of his political debts by appointing a few territorial officers. Less than four years later, he needed an additional state to assure passage of a constitutional amendment in the U.S. Senate and to give the Republican party a few more electoral votes in the 1864 presidential election. So he pushed for and gained admission to the Union for a region that had barely begun to be settled.

Thus Nevada was born prematurely, with far less preparation for statehood than most of its elder sisters. It consisted of only a few mining towns and ranching centers, most of them inhabited by a few dozen or perhaps a few hundred itinerant frontiersmen, scattered across a region as large as the United Kingdom. It was a "pocket borough" from the beginning, the creation of a president and a Congress willing to stretch the provisions of the Constitution to win some short-term, although probably justifiable, political objectives. Notwithstanding the questionable nature of its birth, Nevada became heir to its share of the patrimony and patronage of the federal system. Its two senators were at least numerically equal to their colleagues from New York or Massachusetts, and they quickly became accustomed to the practice of using their votes to gain favors for their remote constituency.

There was still a strong belief in state sovereignty across the land in those years, notwithstanding the fact that the fundamental states-rights doctrines had been discredited by the likes of John C. Calhoun and the secessionists. While Nevadans, in their 1864 constitutional convention, submitted to conditions imposed by Congress and proclaimed their "paramount allegiance" to the federal Union, they came to their condition of statehood convinced that a large measure of local sovereignty remained to them. After all, the spokesmen in Washington from these newest, far western states—California in 1850, Oregon in 1859, and Nevada in 1864—were distinct and remote from the main corpus of the federal Union in a way that the Old South never was. They were separated from their nearest sister states by a thousand miles or more of prairie, mountains, and desert. Long after its admission to the Union, Nevada continued to be a hinterland in the minds of easterners and of its own citizens. Even as California became more sophisticated, famous, and popular, Nevada became more provincial. When its mining bonanza of the 1860s and 1870s fizzled, it did not have, like its fortunate sister to the west, other great resources of water, rich land, forests, and ocean to fall back upon. It was the runt among the states, and its politicians were frequently paranoid and defensive.[4]

The basic problem was that Nevada continued to be essentially a one-industry state; when mining was in the doldrums, it had no dependable alternative. Even the new economic opportunities that appeared at the beginning of the twentieth century, the discovery of new ore bodies at Tonopah, at Goldfield, and near Ely, did not significantly alter the pattern. The dependency on the price of metals and on federal monetary policy continued and, in fact, increased as the twentieth century advanced. The rangelands were valuable, but the markets for livestock were hundreds of miles away, and freight costs were excessive. The Newlands Reclamation Project on the Truckee and Carson rivers—the first of its kind to be financed with federal dollars and the brainchild of Congressman Francis G. Newlands—provided a transfusion for the west-central region of the state, but little more. In 1940, Nevada had an even smaller percentage of the nation's population than it had had seventy years earlier—less than one-tenth of 1 percent.

The Four Nevadas

There were four sub-Nevadas forty years ago, denominated by history and recognized by the local citizenry. To some extent they survived in the early 1980s, but they were gradually being amalgamated into a different culture. Let us reflect briefly on the four zones and then return to take testimony from witnesses on each of them.

We shall begin by ignoring most county boundary lines; in most cases they make no sense, drawn as they were for long-antiquated political purposes. Let us call the four sub-Nevadas (1) the Carson-Truckee region, (2) the Humboldt region, (3) the mining region, and (4) Clark County. The borders between them are not quite clear and some towns belong to more than one zone, but it will help us to understand the transitions of the 1940–1980 era if we divide the state in this manner.

First, in historical and economic terms, is the Carson-Truckee region, embracing the two river systems that bear these names and part of the Walker River basin as well. These little waterways, together with the mountains and valleys through which they flow, were Nevada's birthplace, where the first permanent mines, towns, and ranches were located. Draw a semicircle east of the Sierra Nevada with Carson City as its center, with its radius extending about sixty miles northward and eastward, and you have the Carson-Truckee zone. Rising just off-center near the middle of this arc are the rocky slopes of Mount Davidson, providing an exalted perch for Virginia City, whose bonanza-era memories and values still echo throughout the state.

Fewer than 50,000 people, nearly half the state's population, lived in this region in 1940, and most of these resided in Reno and Sparks. When outsiders spoke of Nevada, it was this region they usually meant. The little agricultural communities of Minden-Gardnerville, Yerington, Smith Valley, Fernley, and Fallon were important in the local context, but they were known to almost no one outside the Sagebrush State.

The second unit of the state is the region of the Humboldt River basin, including Elko, Wells, Winnemucca, Battle Mountain, and Lovelock. One would be tempted to call this northern Nevada if that expression had not been widely preempted in recent years by the Carson-Truckee region. Let us be content to call this the Humboldt district, remembering that we are referring to the river valley and not to the county of that name. This was the region of rangeland and great ranches, opened for economic development by the building of the transcontinental railroad in the 1860s. Cattle, sheep, and trains had been the primary economic assets for seventy years; as of 1940, fewer than 20,000 people had been counted here by the census takers. The main railroad and highway through these towns, then as now, connected them with Reno and—far to the east—Salt Lake City.

East of Carson-Truckee and south of Humboldt, stretching across central Nevada, is the third region, embracing nearly half the state and unbroken by any river worthy of the title. It is not easy to give a name to this section, because it is not so clearly a unit as the first two. But it would be most accurate to call it the mining zone, because nearly all of the main towns were established by the mining booms. Here one finds, even today, only about twenty towns. Austin, Eureka, Pioche, Tonopah, Ely, Goldfield, and Hawthorne each had a few hundred citizens and a courthouse, and an enumeration of these county seats in this vast area nearly exhausts the list of communities with more than 500 people. There were a few railroad towns—Caliente, Mina, and East Ely—and a handful of tiny farming communities clustered around remote springs. Only two or three of these had as many as 1,000 people; most were much smaller.

Then, in the extreme bottom of the Nevada wedge, there is that other district, which has transformed the values, the politics, and the economy of the state since 1940. We may call this the Las Vegas triangle or—to be technically and politically accurate—Clark County. This is a distinct geographical province, drier, hotter, much lower in elevation, in the Mohave Desert rather than the Basin-and-Range ecological province. It was an afterthought as far as Nevada was concerned, not attached to the state until two years after admission to the Union and not organized as a separate county until 1909. Las Vegas did not become a town until 1905, when the Los Angeles–Salt Lake railroad was built through the valley; previously it had been a Mormon mission station (in the 1850s) and a ranch. Las Vegas was so far distant from its sister county seats that it seemed almost to be in a different jurisdiction. For a quarter century it

HUMBOLDT REGION

• WINNEMUCCA
               • ELKO
• BATTLE
  MOUNTAIN

• LOVELOCK

• **RENO**
  • FALLON   • AUSTIN • EUREKA
• VIRGINIA CITY
▲ **CARSON CITY**   • ELY
  • YERINGTON
MINDEN

CARSON-
TRUCKEE   • HAWTHORNE   *MINING REGION*
REGION

            • TONOPAH
                         • PIOCHE
           • GOLDFIELD

The Four
Nevadas

Approx. 110,000 sq. miles
1940: 110,000 people
1980: 801,000 people

CLARK
COUNTY
LAS VEGAS
      •
HENDERSON •
     BOULDER
     CITY

0   50   100   150

SCALE IN MILES

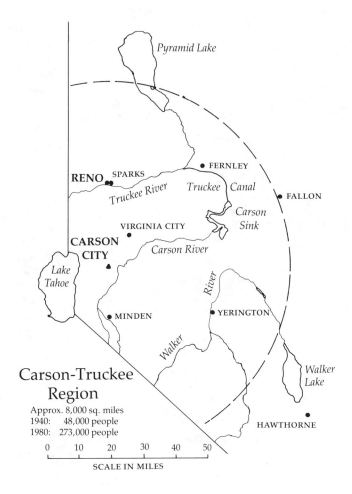

Pyramid Lake

● FERNLEY

RENO ● SPARKS   *Truckee River*   *Truckee Canal*   ● FALLON

VIRGINIA CITY ●   *Carson Sink*

CARSON CITY ▲   *Carson River*

Lake Tahoe

● MINDEN   *Walker River*   ● YERINGTON

Walker Lake

Carson-Truckee Region

Approx. 8,000 sq. miles
1940:   48,000 people
1980: 273,000 people

0   10   20   30   40   50

SCALE IN MILES

● HAWTHORNE

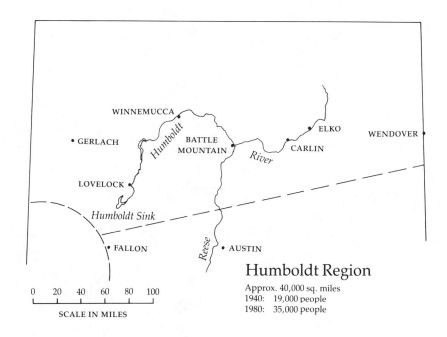

WINNEMUCCA
• GERLACH
Humboldt
BATTLE
MOUNTAIN
ELKO
WENDOVER •
River
CARLIN
LOVELOCK
Humboldt Sink
Reese
• FALLON
• AUSTIN

Humboldt Region

Approx. 40,000 sq. miles
1940:   19,000 people
1980:   35,000 people

0   20   40   60   80   100
SCALE IN MILES

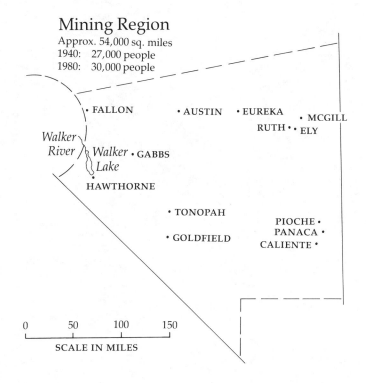

Mining Region

Approx. 54,000 sq. miles
1940:   27,000 people
1980:   30,000 people

• FALLON   • AUSTIN   • EUREKA
                                    • MCGILL
                            RUTH • • ELY
Walker
River *Walker* • GABBS
         Lake
         HAWTHORNE

• TONOPAH
                        PIOCHE •
                        PANACA •
• GOLDFIELD   CALIENTE •

0   50   100   150
SCALE IN MILES

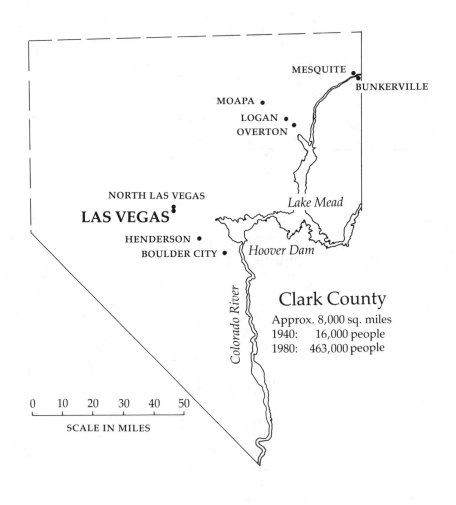

MESQUITE •
BUNKERVILLE

MOAPA •

LOGAN •
OVERTON

NORTH LAS VEGAS

LAS VEGAS •

HENDERSON •
BOULDER CITY •

Lake Mead

Hoover Dam

Colorado River

Clark County

Approx. 8,000 sq. miles
1940:   16,000 people
1980: 463,000 people

0   10   20   30   40   50

SCALE IN MILES

shared the southern triangle with a half-dozen little Mormon villages, a misplaced mining camp, and its railroad—the hottest, least attractive, most distant outback of the poorest state. It provided few participants for the state's political games, few students to its university, and little revenue to its treasury.

But this forgotten corner had possibilities most Nevadans of the northern regions only faintly recognized. For one thing, it bordered on the Colorado River, and the building of Boulder (Hoover) Dam in the 1930s meant payrolls, an unprecedented source of water, and cheap hydroelectric power. It also meant this section of Nevada had opportunities for industrial and commercial development much greater than anything available upstate.

In 1940, Clark County—Nevada's youngest region in terms of settlement—was also its smallest in population. It had only about 16,000 people, most of whom lived in Las Vegas. Yet, even at this stage, Las Vegans were quickly learning the techniques that had made Virginia City and Reno infamous.

A Frontier Legacy

Judged by most of the social standards of the 1980s, the Nevada of 1940 was a quaint place indeed. Although the outside world frowned upon its tolerance of gambling and prostitution, its people saw nothing particularly odd about the rustic values of the frontier from which it was the immediate descendent.

We can best begin our profile of Nevada in 1940 by using the statistics of the U.S. Census Bureau, which every ten years provides a still-life picture of the states.[5] Of the 110,247 people then living in Nevada, more than 104,000 were white—about 95 percent. The various Indian groups numbered 4,747—or about 4 percent—and blacks 664—or about half of 1 percent. Nevada had traditionally drawn a high proportion of its population from abroad,[6] but in 1940 only about 10 percent—or 11,000—of its residents were foreign-born, and most of them were from Canada and northern Europe. Men outnumbered women by about three to two; in the mining camps and ranching areas the imbalance was even greater.

The demographic studies for 1940 showed that Nevada had about 48,000 people over fourteen years of age in the labor force. About 16,000 of these worked in mining, metallurgy, and allied operations, so it was still predominantly a mining state in the twilight of the Great

Depression. About 6,300 people were employed in agriculture, and a like number in "Public emergency work," a euphemism for the New Deal's programs for putting people on a makeshift government payroll. There were fewer than 2,300 employed in "Government," and adding up such categories as "Eating and drinking places," "Hotels and lodging places," and "Amusement recreation, and related services," we get a figure of about 4,200. Many of these places were the saloons where the miners and ranchers found their diversions; a few of them were the "stockades" just off main street where the whorehouses were more or less confined.

Even those communities that fancied themselves as "cities" had fewer people than a local neighborhood in the metropolitan areas of the 1980s. The census takers found only five "cities" in Nevada in 1940—places with more than 2,500 residents:

Reno	21,317
Las Vegas	8,422
Sparks	5,318
Ely	4,140
Elko	4,094

Perhaps if heads had been counted slightly differently and if local township boundaries had not been so rigid, Carson City (2,478) and Winnemucca (2,485) would have made the list as well.

The most revealing profile of the state in the early 1940s was provided by Richard Lillard in his *Desert Challenge: An Interpretation of Nevada*. He found it to be a place of contradictions and contrasts, out of step with much of the rest of the nation:

> Seen by a Californian or a New Yorker Nevada is unorthodox, impious, backward, and undeveloped, yet hospitable, individualistic, romantic. It is the home state for extremes—the smallest population, the biggest public domain, the greatest dryness, the largest proportion of men to women, the highest per capita income. It is everything or nothing, best or worst . . .[7]

Lillard provided us with several verbal portraits of Nevada towns, and there is lasting value in a number of these. He accorded Reno and Las Vegas about the same amount of attention as Virginia City and Goldfield, and his summation of the pretensions of the former is memorable:

> The two largest communities of Nevada are respectable, bumptious, and decadent. Each is a village, a frontier outpost, and a sophisticated cos-

mopolis. Each dominates an end of Nevada. They differ only in size and proportion. With its 23,000 inhabitants Reno is more the cosmopolis. Las Vegas, a quarter as large, is more the frontier town.[8]

These communities were not far removed, in 1942, from the early traditions of the state, and although there was a certain amount of "western posing" among the bellhops, lawyers, and merchants, there were genuine links to the mining camp heritage. The early-day boxing matches, the divorce trade, the more or less open prostitution, and the gambling that shocked or titillated much of the rest of the country were recognized by Lillard as natural continuations of the mining frontier. Although the book was not primarily an apology for Nevada, it provided an extended explanation of the state's nonconforming social practices. While Nevada had been much "scorned and exploited" by outsiders, it had been virtually forced to assume its life of easy virtue. Lillard summarized:

> The ironical side of the whole assault by Americans on the reputation of Nevada is that they themselves are responsible for whatever evils really existed. Statehood was thrust on the territory during a crucial year of the Civil War. It was men and women from all the states and territories who crowded into early Washoe to give it its turbulent, unregulated life. . . . The big prize fights were attended by men coming in special trains from both coasts, from states that prohibited fights. The gamblers of early days learned their trade elsewhere, and the profitable modern revival of gambling is made possible by tourists and temporary visitors. And as for divorce, Easterners first exploited it and they are the ones who have made it a major state industry. Nevadans did not create most of the conditions that have held back development of the state. If the state is disreputable, it is not to blame. If it has been unworthy of sovereignty, its fellow states and their citizens have been the unwitting cause, and they should have proposed aid, not extinction.[9]

Never has Nevada had a more effective justification for its wayward social philosophy. One senses, in reading the statements made about Nevada by its own citizens in the early 1940s, that they hoped to overcome their unfortunate reputation, to become respectable, and to join the American mainstream. Hardly anyone would have predicted at that time that the state's business and political representatives would begin to promote its vices and to institutionalize them more fully.

We were indeed innocents, those of us who were coming of age in Nevada in the 1940s. We were proud of the frontier heritage and thought of building fine new American cities on this land that our ancestors were still in the process of conquering from the wilderness. We did not waste much of our youthful energy worrying about the distant wars or the criminals who operated in remote places like Chicago, about whom we knew, of course, from the movies that played in the old Opera House. We did not recognize until many years afterward that both the war and the mobsters had become our neighbors.

CHAPTER 2

THE FOUR NEVADAS REVISITED: 1980

THE FOUR NEVADAS have gone their separate ways in these two-score years. The state has set some American records for growth in Las Vegas and Reno; on the other hand, there are entire counties, some of which are as large as a New England state, that have been virtually dormant, and this magnifies the diversity that already existed between the regions. And the gap seems to become wider as the years pass.

The Carson-Truckee Region

For more than a decade after 1940, Reno held its traditional place as Nevada's foremost city. During three-quarters of a century, it has presented two contrasting faces to the outside world. It was both the "concentrated little Byzantium" described by Max Miller (who seems to have gathered most of his impressions in the saloons) and "The City of Trembling Leaves," the bucolic oasis described in Walter Van Tilburg Clark's sentimental 1945 novel of that name. Until well after the midpoint of this century, Reno's conservative ordinances kept virtually all of the gambling establishments confined to four or five downtown blocks. There was an official "red line" area beyond which the casinos would not be licensed. When Oscar Lewis published his account of the *Sagebrush Casinos* in 1953, he reported, as many of his journalistic predecessors had done, that visitors were often surprised to find that the gambling dens and the notorious divorce business operated in a "typical American community of the more progressive sort, with evidences of enterprise and civic pride everywhere visible."[1] The tourists occasionally assumed that if the social vices that had made Reno infamous were somehow enclosed in an average-looking city with prosperous homes, a picturesque little university, and numerous churches, it could not be as bad as it had been represented in the sensational press. Its location in a beautiful valley at the eastern edge of the Sierra enabled Reno to provide an attractive, almost deceptive, wrapping for a package of dubious content.

Until the 1970s, when the red-line policy collapsed and the casinos spread like an ugly rash along some of the attractive old streets and into the outskirts that had previously been limited to residential, agricultural, and small business uses, it was possible to believe that Reno was in control of its gambling houses, rather than the other way around.

Walter Clark, one of the few Nevada "insiders" who made a meaningful contribution to the literature of the West and won a national reputation, published an affectionate impression of Reno at the end of the 1940s, and he still found it a charming place. To him it was both "the state big city and the national small town." It was not large enough to be self-sufficient and was therefore highly dependent on its distant contacts and on the tourist business, but, on the other hand, it stood in about the same relationship to the state of Nevada that New York City did to the state of New York.[2] The average Renoite, he said, felt a close kinship not only with his own little city but with those other towns scattered across the sagebrush valleys and rocky hills to the east and south. There was a unity, a symbiotic relationship, between Reno and the hinterland (including Las Vegas) that had existed since pioneer days. "The whole state is his [i.e., the Renoite's] community personally, not just politically," Clark concluded. "He'll be going down to Vegas for the Helldorado, and to Carson for Admission Day, and to Fallon for the Fair. He has seen the state with his own eyes, and it is huge, but geometrically simple and easy to remember. It is his, literally."

Reno was, in those years, a *polis* in the classical Greek sense of the term. It more or less ran its own affairs, and drew its share of young aspirants to fame and fortune from the adjacent Great Basin wilderness and developed in them a regional loyalty, which they seldom betrayed. One could easily meet the people of importance in the local *agora*—one of the casino bars—and talk about matters of state. Within a two-block area of downtown Reno in 1950 were the offices of the two U.S.

senators and the congressman, and they played the political game as though Reno were the nucleus of the universe.[3]

In 1940, the tourists had hardly discovered Carson City, and vice versa. The capital city was not yet "urban" by the standards of the Bureau of Census because it lacked 2,500 residents, and most of the important state offices could be accommodated in the capitol building, which had been erected in 1870, and in the Heroes Memorial Building across the street. The tree-shaded residential streets were more suggestive of rural Ohio than of the Great Basin. Many of its finer homes were of pre-1900 construction, and the interior of the Governor's Mansion still reflected the heavily curtained, darkly varnished tastes of the first ladies who had resided there in the Victorian era.

Virginia City likewise stood as a testimonial to faded pseudoelegance, but it was in a much poorer state of repair than Carson. The buildings along C Street might have been appropriate as a studio-set for a Hollywood western movie if they had not appeared to be about to tumble down the gulch into Six-Mile Canyon. But the bartenders and their local patrons were already discovering that there was profit—or at least a sustaining livelihood and an occasional free drink—to be had for trading in stories and supposed relics of the bonanza days. The Comstock Lode had been much written up, and even in that era before hyper-advertising, motorists enjoyed driving up the steep Geiger Grade from Reno to see the source of all those millions. Lillard and a score of other writers testified that the residents of the Comstock still had faith that there was yet another bonanza to be discovered beneath Mount Davidson. But they did not find it underground.

Out through the mining country, this yearning for another Comstock Lode was more intense than in Virginia City itself, because the businesspeople outside Reno-Carson-Virginia had not yet learned about tourism. Even up north in the Humboldt country, where there had never been an important gold and silver boom, the quest for a bonanza was a common itch. Dale Morgan, the Berkeley scholar who wrote his impressions of that basin for the Rivers of America series in the early 1940s, commented:

> The hills that roll north and south from the sundering westward thrust of the Humboldt Valley are a common denominator of life. Everybody is a prospector, by profession or by inclination. When out in the hills on any

business, a man has an eye for the terrain around; and when vacations attend the normal course of the new urban life in the Humboldt Valley, a man is more likely to go prospecting than to go fishing. . . .

This land has, after all, the memory of the Comstock, that incandescence of bygone years. The Comstock symbolizes all the wealth ever found in Nevada's mountains, and the abundance of its life—its nervous energy, its overflowing vitality, its exciting gusto—is something more than a land's memory of its youth.[4]

And so it was in the Pioche of my childhood, where my father worked in the mines about ten hours a day, six days a week, and observed the sabbath by prospecting. With Mother and four or five of us and a picnic, he would set out for the ridges fifty miles northward, often to check out the gold claims that had been staked by his father; while he prospected, we younger ones played at doing "assessment work," which under Nevada mining law was necessary to hold the claim. He was always, as he said, either a foot from a million dollars or a million feet from a dollar, but it did not matter much, because the excitement was in the search.

The new bonanza, however, was not in the mountains; it was to be found in the valleys, especially in the Truckee Meadows (Reno) at that stage. There the "clubs" were learning to lure a gambling clientele as never before. Raymond I. Smith, the founder of Harolds Club in Reno, had begun to advertise his establishment on billboards across the nation and had introduced young women as dealers behind the green-felt tables where only men had been considered appropriate earlier. Soon other club operators in Reno—and in due course in Carson City, in Virginia City, at Lake Tahoe, and in Las Vegas—followed suit.

In the Carson-Truckee region, the payoff was impressive in the next forty years—if we may consider it from a narrow commercial point of view. Although there was no new productive industry or human service of any consequence, the number of permanent residents increased five- to ten-fold. Compare, for example, the population records for 1940 and 1980, using, in this case, the township figures, not merely the city tabulations, so that the suburbs may be taken into account.[5]

	1940	1980
Reno	24,901	137,542
Sparks	5,901	53,230
Carson City	3,209	32,022
Tahoe (South)	—	5,386
Carson Valley	2,056	14,053
Yerington	2,103	5,050

These are miniscule population statistics by the standards of the twentieth century, but they reveal a pattern that has occurred frequently in the "underdeveloped world"—outskirts and outbacks that were only recently wastelands and have lately been sprouting subdivisions.

On the eastern edge of the Carson-Truckee province, where a blending with the central Nevada mining region begins, the communities of Fallon and Hawthorne enjoyed or endured a halfway status. They had been on the fringe of the mining country and were off the main tourist thoroughfares. They benefited from some of the federal largess that came to the Great Basin as a result of the military preparations of the 1930s and 1940s. Fallon, which came into existence as a result of the Newlands project for irrigating desert lands in the early 1900s, got a new economic transfusion with the building of a naval air station during World War II. Hawthorne, an old railroad town and supply point for adjacent mining districts, had been chosen in the 1920s as the site for a naval (later army) ammunition depot and managed to survive and to expand slightly on the strength of federal dollars spent for military preparedness. The demographic changes there were much more modest.

	1940	1980
Fallon and area	5,317	13,917
Hawthorne	1,229	5,166

So Nevada's small communities outside the Truckee Meadows showed relatively little change in these forty years if one considers only the bare statistics. Much of the old Nevada remained intact in those parts, even as the new yeast worked in Las Vegas and Reno.

Borrasca in the Mines

Virginia City and Gold Hill sit in the tiara of the Carson-Truckee district, high on the slopes of Mount Davidson, but by 1940 they had lost most of their luster. Not only the depression of the 1880s but also the Great Depression of the 1930s had seemed to confirm that the dry rot that afflicted their buildings was a fitting metaphor for the economic condition of the Comstock Lode and other old mining districts. The hard-rock quartzite mining of pioneer days, which had been elevated to a fine art in the Comstock shafts and stopes, was virtually dead, and so it seemed also throughout the Mining zone. Let us consider the statistics for the towns where the extraction of metals from the earth had been the primary industry before the 1940s.[6]

	1940	1980
Virginia City/Gold Hill	1,216	1,503
Austin	580	436
Eureka	705	798
Ely (incl. McGill)	10,883	7,559
Pioche	1,605	794
Tonopah	2,417	2,680
Goldfield	554	777

In each of these courthouse towns, the mining industry that had created and sustained them from the beginning was dormant. The promotional brochures produced by the state government and the occasional propaganda supplements issued by the local newspapers spoke repeatedly of the unusual economic opportunities that awaited the investor, but a close reading of most of these often left the impression that fresh air and friendly people were the most obvious assets. This "Other Nevada," as Robert Laxalt called the outlying counties in a widely read article published in *National Geographic*,[7] was economically moribund, except in the towns that had been able to make the transition from industries that exploit the earth to those that exploit the tourists.

Well before 1940, a fundamental change had begun to occur in the mining industry. In the boom years of the 1870s and again in the 1900–1914 period, the state had known relative prosperity because of the success of the gold and silver mining districts. But during and after the First World War, the nonprecious metals replaced the precious ores as the mainstay of the economy. The copper mines and smelter of the Ely-Ruth-McGill district became the most significant mineral producers within Nevada's borders, and the sustained production of "low-grade" ores there ultimately yielded a dollar value that exceeded the total gold and silver output of the Comstock Lode. Other industrial metals such as lead, zinc, manganese, magnesite, and tungsten drew more of the attention of the mining companies, which also began to tap vast deposits of mundane metals needed for construction. The senior mining men were somewhat slow to acknowledge it, but the day of the bonanza ore bodies, located near the surface of the earth in "high-grade" pockets, was past. This was becoming evident as early as the 1920s, but the instincts of the gold and silver prospector lingered well beyond mid-century.

When gold and silver mining underwent a revival in the 1970s because of a rapid rise in the prices of these metals on the world market, the developers who opened the new mines or reopened the old ones were seldom the local people who had waited so long for the return of the bonanza. Rather, they were usually Texan or eastern or Canadian capitalists, and their methods had little in common with those of the early lode miners. Typical of the new techniques was the work of a Texas-based company that moved into Gold Hill and gouged a massive hole into the side of Mount Davidson, obliterating much of the natural and historical attractiveness of the site.

Gold and silver mining had become the invalid of the mining business. The prices of both metals had been artificially propped up by federal law in the early 1930s, and a policy that had been designed as a crutch in those hard times became an obstacle to the industry in the inflationary era that followed the Second World War, because for more than a quarter-century the prices of the precious metals were not allowed to fluctuate. Also, most of the older mining towns that had prospered in the past—Virginia City, Austin, Eureka, Pioche, Tonopah, Goldfield— watched their mineshafts collapse, their equipment decay and fall into hands of junk dealers, and their young people leave to seek employment in the cities. The always risky mining business seemed more economically doubtful than ever.

In addition, during the boom days, all of these camps had enjoyed the services of a railroad. In most of the larger mining districts, tracks had been swiftly laid to allow the steam locomotives to carry passengers, freight, and ore between the towns and main transcontinental lines. But between 1937 and 1950, the most famous of these spur lines into the mining districts ceased operating. Their owners tore up their rails for scrap and surrendered their roadbeds to the reconquering desert. One by one the pioneering lines died like unwatered fruit trees on an abandoned homestead—the Nevada Central Line into Austin in 1937, the Eureka & Palisade in 1938, the Virginia & Truckee between Carson City and Virginia City in 1939, the Tonopah & Tidewater in 1940, and Tonopah & Goldfield in 1946. The most famous of all, the Virginia & Truckee, continued to offer service between Reno and Carson City until 1950, but it too succumbed to the economic realities, and most of its equipment went to Hollywood or to the scrap metal dealers.[8]

So the mining camps lost the conduits of steam and iron that had once carried the ore or bullion outward and commerce of the great world inward, and the paved highways that were supposed to be their replacements did not provide an adequate substitute. Only Pioche and Ely managed to retain their branch lines into the 1980s, and Pioche lost its link to the transcontinental rails in 1984. The alternative lines of commerce, the freeways that carried the great volume of the traffic in humans and hardware in the last third of the twentieth century, were scores or hundreds of miles away.

The Humboldt Country

Communities along the old Humboldt trail have made the transition to late twentieth century commercialism with greater success than the mining camps have. Lovelock, Winnemucca, Battle Mountain, Elko, and Wells supplemented their cattle-country economies with the tourist dollars that were dropped along Highway 40/Interstate 80. Once again the population figures are informative.

	1940	1980
Lovelock and vicinity	2,713	3,408
Winnemucca	2,708	7,209
Battle Mountain	1,165	3,640
Elko/Carlin	5,636	12,678

While the comparative figures are not completely valid in all cases because of changes in township lines, the general pattern is clear. Where a community had the advantages of an interstate freeway—including the payrolls that resulted from the construction of those arterials in the 1950s, 1960s, and 1970s, and the truckers who used them—it was possible to prosper in a way that the mining towns were unable to do.

Communities like Elko and Winnemucca had become, by 1980, an uneasy blend of the old Nevada and the new. The prevailing values and social attitudes were still those of the postfrontier cattle and railroad towns, staunchly conservative, basically suspicious of the outside. But, on the other hand, they were increasingly prone to rely upon the tourist dollars and more especially on the gambling entrepreneurs. As the co-authors of the foremost history of northeastern Nevada wrote:

> In sharp contrast to the old ways, drums of commercialism beat in increasing rhythm in the desert town of Elko in 1969, as merchants bid for increased business and added dollars. Nite clubs and hotel entertainment no longer meet the standard, "one to which you can take your children," but instead feature "the girls" in topless garb. On special holidays and weekends, Utahans, brought in by hotel-sponsored package deals which include bargain price transportation, meals, drinks, rooms, and shows, crowd Elko.[9]

So it was in several of the towns along the freeway, but if one rambled back and forth across central and northern Nevada in 1980, through the Carson-Truckee areas or the Humboldt Valley or the mining region, one found only two or three new towns of any consequence that did not depend almost entirely on gambling-tourism. (At Lake Tahoe, high in the Sierra Nevada, there were some new communities, and Wendover on the Nevada-Utah border prospered, but these places also grew because of the gambling trade.) The maps and social generalizations about the communities of the 1940s in the northern and central regions often had much validity at the beginning of the penultimate decade of the century. But this was not at all true of Clark County. There, an almost totally different Nevada had come into existence, with new cities, new industries, and new values that were hardly comprehended in the northern towns.

The New Bonanza in the South

In 1940, Las Vegas was much like the town it had been thirty years earlier, in its fledgling days as a railroad division point. It was confined within an area of twelve square miles, which embraced the depot, the old Mormon Fort, and two short business streets. One could walk anywhere in town within an hour. The Works Projects Administration guide to Nevada, published in 1940 in connection with one of the anti-Depression programs, summarized:

> Within the city, whose business center is close to a new and very modern Union Pacific station at the head of Fremont Street, are Old Town—West Las Vegas—where many of the simpler houses stand; North Las Vegas, a suburb where large houses have been built; and an inner residential district with many modern homes. Beyond this fringe, on all sides, is the desert.[10]

As of 1940, neither the Westside, where the black population was beginning to congregate, nor North Las Vegas was significant enough to warrant separate consideration by the census takers. The opening of that new Union Pacific passenger depot seemed easily to be the most important event of the year. Charles P. "Pop" Squires, who had been publishing the *Las Vegas Age* for thirty years and who still featured the news of the social clubs and lodges on the front page, regarded the building of an air-conditioned station as a matter of historic consequence and as a gamble that might fail if the locals did not patronize the railroad. After all, he editorialized, there were depots elsewhere in which bats now roosted because the railroads they had been built to serve were defunct.

He reminded his readership, lest it should forget, that it had a solemn obligation to support the railroad as a dutiful child would its parent: "Having come to life as an offspring of the railroad, this same parent is still our chief source of payroll. Its many activities have enabled us to live and grow as a town."[11] That Squires should have been so cautious and uncertain about the city's future should not surprise us. Southern Nevada had just experienced the economic trauma of the 1930s and had only been able to weather the economic storms because of the building of Boulder Dam on the Colorado River, but this project had been finished; as of 1940, there was no assurance that it would not follow its sister towns to the north into borrasca.

Squires had no way of anticipating that within a year or two a desperate need for magnesium for wartime use would prompt the U.S. government to build a massive plant on the barren flats ten miles south of Las Vegas, or that the Army Air Force would select the little landing field north of town for its most significant fighter training center in the Far West. He had no way of knowing, when Mae West and W. C. Fields visited the town to perform *My Little Chickadee,* or when George Burns and Gracie Allen stopped for a few days to offer their routine, that they were the precursors of a parade of entertainers who would make Las Vegas more popular than Hollywood itself as a place to see the cinema idols in the flesh. And Squires—who, incidentally, lived to be a hundred years old and received a congratulatory telegram from President Dwight D. Eisenhower—certainly could not have anticipated in 1940 the emergence of one of America's 100 largest cities and the infiltration of some of America's most notorious gangsters in his own valley within his lifetime.

Once more, let us consider the raw census statistics, this time for the townships of Clark County.

	1940	1980
Las Vegas	10,389	350,511
North Las Vegas	—	71,605
Henderson	—	24,334
Boulder City	2,959	10,059
Bunkerville	287	492
Logan	358	1,087
Mesquite	515	922
Moapa	345	702
Overton	692	1,752

This tabulation suggests two obvious conclusions—that about two-thirds of Nevada's population growth of the past four decades has occurred in the Las Vegas Valley, and that the small Mormon towns along the Moapa and Virgin rivers (the last five listed above) have had approximately the same kind of demographic stability—or stagnation—as the mining towns to the north.

The growth of Las Vegas has been accompanied by a southward migration from these little Mormon towns and from the valleys and mountains of the mining districts as well. Las Vegas became, in this period, the metropolis to which the restless and the ambitious often gravitated, just as Virginia City had done in the 1860s and Reno a generation or two later. The men and women from rural regions provided a large share of the social and political leadership as Las Vegas grew. Thus there has been more continuity from the old Nevada to the new than the bare statistics would suggest, notwithstanding the fact that the great majority of the new Nevadans came from outside the state.

So much has been written about Las Vegas that it would be fair to ask whether there is anything meaningful left to be said, but most of what has been published has dealt with the gambling business, the connections with the underworld crime figures, the entertainment world, and the atomic testing program and the other federal activities.[12] We hardly need between these covers another description of the murder of Bugsy Siegel—the first notorious victim of gangland slaying in that city—or yet one more account of the strange behavior of the billionaire Howard Hughes. Eventually we shall have to consider what such men did to and for the state, but for the moment let us confine ourselves to the question of the meaning of the foregoing figures. When the boom of the early 1940s began, the town's promoters emphasized the connections with the frontier West.[13] They promoted the "Helldorado" rodeo as the main annual attraction for visitors. They hired a pseudoprospector and his burro to walk along Fremont Street to charm the visitors and offer himself for photographs with the tourists. The first resort built on the highway toward Los Angeles that eventually became the famous Strip called itself El Rancho Vegas, and a couple of years later it was followed by the Last Frontier. Only later did the names of exotic tropical birds, corporations, and fancy desert themes become popular.

As there was almost no agriculture in the Las Vegas Valley and, before the development of the Basic Magnesium Plant, no important industry besides the railroad, the town's boosters increasingly put their emphasis on Las Vegas as a place where one could enjoy the loose social standards and exhilarations of the Wild West. Whereas Reno had tried to show its respectable face to the outside world even in its heyday as a divorce mill, Las Vegas seemed to relish notoriety. It promoted "glitter gulch"—as the Fremont Street casino cluster was called in the 1940s— and in the early 1950s it was common to see promotional material about the "atomic bonanza." The Chamber of Commerce became at least as important as the city and county governments in setting policies and shaping community priorities.

The city of Las Vegas drafted a master plan in 1944, and there were repeated efforts to guide the growth of the region according to pro-fessional urban planning standards. The planning agencies, however, were usually overruled or ignored by the governing bodies of the various jurisdictions; city and county commissioners often disagreed, and the metropolis sprawled across the sands of the broad valley in a chaotic manner; as a leading student of the city's growth testified, "orderly planning was sacrificed in the name of economic progress."[14] Such amenities as street paving, lighting, and telephone service often lagged behind the ever-growing popular demand, and the schools, the fire departments and police facilities, and the recreational services barely kept pace in the 1940s and 1950s. It was a boom beyond the wildest dreams of even the most imaginative of the mining town boosters of old. City managers and professional planners who were hired to produce orderly growth usually had short tenures.

No city in America was more keenly attuned to the possibilities of tourism in the 1950s. Americans were on the road in that first postwar decade, willing to go much further than ever before for their conventions and vacations. Late in that decade, Las Vegas made its own biggest gamble: it erected a massive convention center capable of handling the largest meetings, and it was estimated that $20 million in revenue— several times the cost of the building—came to the area in the first year of its operation.[15] When "glitter gulch" became overcrowded with casinos, it spread north, south, and east, and when the Strip along the Los Angeles highway seemed to reach out far enough, a second Strip began to emerge along a parallel street. There appeared to be no limit to the amount of capital that could be raised for investment in the Las Vegas action.

The residential subdivisions that sprawled across the valley resem-bled those that spread out from the other rapidly growing southwestern regions, especially in Arizona and California. Lavish mansions and gardens worthy of comparison with those in California and Hawaii rose as though in a fairy-tale fantasy; not far distant, row upon row of twentieth-century ticky-tacky houses brought premium prices.

At the end of the 1950s, as the new convention center was being completed, the Las Vegas Planning Commission examined the city's past and potential development and made some seemingly outrageous twenty-year projections for growth.[16] These proved to be far too conservative. The population had increased about sixfold—from 8,400 within the city limits to about 53,000—between 1940 and 1958. The commission expected the addition of another 65,000 people by 1980; in fact, the population grew by about 110,000. The commission estimated that Clark County would have 370,000 by 1980, but in that year the Bureau of the Census counted more than 461,000. The commission's expectations for the remainder of Nevada were reasonably near the mark, but it failed to put its money on the fast track for Las Vegas itself.[17] When the 1980 census returns had been completed, Nevada had become eligible, for the first time, for a second representative in Congress. For the first 115 years of statehood, it had had only one.

The commission's planners expressed a concern that has continued to be shared by the conservative residents of the area—and of the state at large—for a half-century. Was the community stable? Did it have the economic base to face a time of adversity? It was essentially the same warning that "Pop" Squires had uttered in 1940, although in slightly different dress. After a discreet amount of word shuffling, the 1959 report concluded that the economy was stable, but "unbalanced." Without much elaboration on this distinction, it pronounced not only that there was too great an emphasis on tourism, but that "the tourist economy itself is somewhat out of balance."[18] This undoubtedly meant to convey the idea, which could not be expressed without some caution in Las Vegas by a group of minor bureaucratic planners, that a few large, rich, and vulnerable casinos accounted for too much of the city's business.

But this concern, often expressed in upstate political circles as well as in the more conservative local forums, did not get translated into policy. Until the early 1980s, it seemed that Nevada's tourist-gambling economy was "recession proof." It had continued to grow through all of the various economic slowdowns of the 1960s and 1970s. It looked far better, on the profit-and-loss sheets, than the automobile or steel industries, farming, or—for that matter—mining. But in 1981 and 1982, for the first time since the exhilarating expansion of the 1940s began, something appeared to be seriously wrong. Casino managers and taxi drivers, those bellwethers of local morale, had often cried "wolf" before when the growth pattern had been only slightly less than they had expected, but this time the revenues from tourism actually fell. It was "Snake eyes for Las Vegas," *Newsweek* magazine reported.[19] Later that year, the unemployment rate exceeded 10 percent statewide.

By all the traditional measures, Las Vegas had entered the 1980s as optimistic about future growth as ever. Forty years of continuous expansion had created an expectation of rising indexes and ever-increasing winnings. A semiofficial pamphlet called *Las Vegas Perspectives* appeared in 1981 with a profile of the community based upon the most reliable evidence available.[20] It found Las Vegas to be a predominantly "youthful community," with a much higher percentage of residents between the ages of twenty and forty-five than most metropolitan areas and with relatively few older citizens. This reflected the fact that, although the casino-resort business often catered to an older clientele, it most often got its employees from the ranks of the young adults. Las Vegas, therefore, might be regarded as an instrument for funneling some excess capital from the accounts of the idle, elderly rich to the younger set that had not found productive employment elsewhere and had therefore come to Vegas for quick money.

In spite of the repeated efforts to diversify the economy, Las Vegas was more tied to the gambling-tourist economy than ever before in the early 1980s. The statistics on construction emphasized this point. A tabulation of 100 important building projects, recently completed or underway in 1981, totaled nearly $1.6 billion, and the large majority of these were casino-hotel or resort facilities. One of the largest, a $26.5 million university sports arena, had been funded for the interests of the tourist economy rather than for any purposes of higher education. Although Clark County had a 53 percent share of the state's tourist industry and more than half the state's population, it had only about a third of the manufacturing business, less than 6 percent of its agriculture, and less than 3 percent of its mining.[21] It was therefore especially vulnerable to the kind of recession that occurred in 1981–1982.

A year later, the recession seemed to have eased, and Las Vegas—a city of short memories because it is so young and full of transients— seemed not to have learned any lesson from the hiatus in its growth. There were some suburbs, however, with separate community orientations, which might have been more alert to alternatives, or more eager to find them.

North Las Vegas and Henderson, which did not exist on the official maps in 1940, have been seeking a place in the sun outside the penumbra of Las Vegas for at least three decades. North Las Vegas is easily the most populous "new" city in the state in this era, but it is almost entirely unknown outside the immediate region. There was a voting precinct and a post office there in the 1930s, but little more. In 1980, it was the third largest urban unit in Nevada. It had sprawled along North Main Street and around Nellis Air Force Base, and its people, mobile though most of them were through the years, inherited and transmitted a separatist allegiance that extended back in time nearly a hundred years. In pioneer days, there had been a different ranch—the Kyle Place—distinct from the Stewart Ranch that embraced the old Las Vegas Mission. Although there was no discernible continuity in peoples and no geographical boundary, the residents of the two places habitually thought of themselves as separate from one another, and therefore it was so.

Civic leaders for North Las Vegas intermittently sought to cultivate a sense of neighborhood pride, but the effort met with only modest success. The site was called Hooverville during the Great Depression, as many other poor districts were, and it never quite escaped the heritage of poverty. People still occasionally referred to it as North Town in 1980. It remained a satellite of both Las Vegas and the Nellis Air Force Base, embracing neighborhoods of low-cost housing and some warehousing and light industry attracted by the availability of the railroad.

In 1973—some twenty-seven years after it first affirmed its separate existence (it was incorporated in 1946)—North Las Vegas indulged itself in a "Community Analysis and Evaluation Program," which is the urban equivalent of a medical and psychiatric examination. The aspiring city was not unhealthy, but it had some problems with its self-image. While the analysis did not produce much new information, it endowed what was known with a statistical garland. North Las Vegas had more poor people, more working wives, more blacks and Hispanics, and fewer cultural amenities than its neighbors.[22] It recorded that there was not a single "new car agency in or even near North Las Vegas." The city did not have enough retail outlets for wearing apparel and pharmaceuticals; it was deficient in movie theaters, and it had none of the glamorous advantages of the Strip or Casino Row downtown. And there was not one gourmet restaurant in the city.[23]

The "Community Analysis" report sounded in places much like the lamentations of a mining camp in borrasca, but unlike the gold and silver towns that had faded when the pay streaks had pinched out, North Las Vegas had continued to grow, regardless of the number of people who left. In 1940, it had not been on the maps; in 1980, there were more than 70,000 people in the township and nearly 43,000 in the city. The community college was serving 9,000 students, and it was a suburban unit more organically active than most of the state of Nevada had been a half-century earlier. But more than any other Nevada community, it was an indentured servant, surrounded on three sides by its metropolitan master.

In the quadrant of the valley opposite North Las Vegas, the other vigorous new city arose, also in the 1940s. Henderson had from the beginning a *raison d' être* and an identity of its own. Separated from the center of Las Vegas by more than ten miles, it came into existence within a few months of the beginning of World War II because the United States government was aware of a desperate shortage of magnesium among the foes of Nazi Germany and Japan, and it decided to develop a large deposit of the metal in western Nevada and to process it in southern Nevada near the abundant water and inexpensive electrical power of Boulder Dam. Exciting stories about the stealing and transmission of secret Nazi plans were associated with the creation of the Basic Magnesium Plant.[24] Shortly before the United States was drawn into war by the bombing of Pearl Harbor, a contract had been let to build a huge magnesium refining center at an estimated cost of $60 million and to transport water from Lake Mead across the mountains into the Las Vegas Valley for its operation. Within eighteen months, more than ten thousand people were working at various phases of construction and production—more than had ever been employed in the greatest booms in any of Nevada's mining camps. After only about a year of full production, the Henderson facility had produced a surplus of magnesium for weapons; by the end of the war, the government was ready to dismantle or scrap the industrial complex.

Timely action by Nevada political leaders prevented this from occurring. The state government bought the plant on easy terms and resold most of its facilities to private manufacturers—producers of insecticides, fuels, titanium and other metals, lime, and domestic products. Southern Nevada had its first genuinely productive industrial complex not immediately related to and dependent upon mining. Henderson grew into a town of 5,550 by 1950, doubled its size by 1960, and doubled it again by 1980, when it had more than 24,000 residents. It was, in brief, as large as Reno had been in 1940, and its incorporated municipal area extended across seventy square miles.

Henderson had a broader industrial and commercial diversification than any other community in Nevada. While some industrial manufacturers of the 1940s that were located in Henderson had modified their operations in response to changing economic and environmental

Reno, ca. 1940.

Las Vegas, ca. 1960.

Pioche, ca. 1939.

Ranching in northeastern Nevada.

Mizpah Mine, Tonopah, late 1930s.

Las Vegas Convention Center.

The Atomic Age, 1950s.

conditions, Henderson continued to attract new and small industries of various kinds. A clothing manufacturer, a shoe company, an electronics company, battery manufacturers, a candy maker, and different kinds of metal processors located in the area. The city did not overlook the possibilities of tourism—it completed the construction of a million-dollar convention center in 1981—but it did not stake its future on the tourist business to the extent that other Nevada towns were doing. The city government and the Chamber of Commerce, still optimistic about the prospects for growth in 1981, projected an eventual population of 160,000.[25]

While Henderson retained the boom mentality reminiscent of early Nevada and of Las Vegas, its neighbor Boulder City had adopted a much more sedate attitude. Established in 1932 by the Bureau of Reclamation as a planned community, it became home to many of the professional people responsible for the building and operation of Boulder/Hoover Dam and for the accommodation of the millions of visitors who arrived to see it. Its citizens were initially tenants of the United States; they did not have an opportunity to buy their homes from the government until more than a decade after the completion of the dam. When they did organize a self-governing, incorporated city, they had acquired the habit of careful planning and adopted policies to discourage the kind of urban sprawl that was occurring on the other side of the mountains in the Las Vegas Valley.

Although Boulder City has not entirely escaped the ugly blight that the tourist industries have strewn along the Nevada highways, it has maintained its status as contemporary Nevada's most pleasant example of a well-planned community. The handsome homes on carefully land-scaped terraces, the wide, uncrowded streets, and the conservative southwestern architectural styles testify to a determination of at least one city to turn its back on much of the rampant commercialism that Nevada has come to represent. The city annexed much land in the surrounding hills, not to promote growth as most municipalities had done, but to prevent unwanted expansion. It has often discouraged questionable industries and gambling establishments from locating there on the ground that too much business of that kind would damage the quality of life. It was an odd attitude for a Nevada town, but a refreshing one. The population rose from only about 3,000 to slightly more than 10,000 in the forty years under review here.

When I was a child in Pioche in the late 1930s and Boulder Dam was new (we did not learn to call it Hoover Dam until a decade later, when a

Republican Congress formally approved its intended name), we looked forward with much anticipation to our family visits there. President Roosevelt himself had come to dedicate the dam, and we were encouraged to think of it as one of the wonders of the world, comparable to a pyramid of Egypt, and the oasis of Boulder City with its subtropical greenery was a dazzling sight for desert dwellers.

The older generation was convinced that this dam promised the beginning of the prosperous revival for our mining districts and rangelands nearly two hundred miles to the north. Our parents anticipated the building of power lines to our remote towns, the pumping out of the long-flooded mines, the raising of underground rivers to the surface of our dry valleys, and the return of the bonanza. When we turned on the Boulder Dam power for the first time in 1937, we blew the new fire siren for hours in tribute to the opening of the new era. But we made a few miscalculations about the kind of bonanza that was about to be discovered in our frontier state.

CHAPTER 3

THE STRUGGLES FOR WATER

ONE OF THE OLDEST human enterprises in the Great Basin has been the effort to gather and hold sufficient water to sustain life. From the days of the aboriginal residents who clustered around the shrinking Lake Lahontan, to the Paiutes who performed rain dances, to the earliest white settlers to the first people who diverted the flow of tiny mountain streams, until the day of the large federal reclamation projects and cloud-seeding experiments, the underlying quest for humans living in Nevada has been for enough water to continue the contemporary enterprise—whatever that was—through the next season.

Most of the rivers on which Nevadans rely originate outside the state. The Colorado River has its beginnings hundreds of miles to the north and east, in the Colorado mountains near the Continental Divide. The Truckee, Carson, and Walker rivers all rise in California and draw their sustenance from the snowfall there before delivering their bounty to the most westerly valleys of the Great Basin. Nevada has no real river of its own, except the Humboldt, which in a dry year is so meager that it would not even deserve the designation of "river," if it happened to be anywhere in the eastern part of North America.

How did the driest state in the Union, long notorious for its interminable expanses of desert waste, find the water to sustain its sevenfold increase in population? There was no obvious surplus of water in 1940, except perhaps in the Colorado River, which touched only the southern extreme of the state, but a combination of successful planning and engineering, tedious litigation, and good luck produced fortunate results in some of the driest regions.

Those engineers who made Nevada's basic water decisions between the 1930s and the 1980s were often quite astute in their predictions and warnings. Alfred Merritt Smith, the state engineer, cautioned Las Vegas in the early 1940s when it had only about 10,000 people that it was running out of water, long before most local residents recognized the danger, and he helped to design a forty-year solution. Elsewhere, politicians found money for reclamation projects both within and outside the state to store floodwaters for use during dry periods; Senator Alan Bible, who served in the upper house from 1954 to 1974, was a key figure in this enterprise. Several of the state's lawyers enhanced their careers by litigating water-rights cases, and those who represented Nevada did quite well for their clients. Perhaps most important, between 1940 and 1980, Nevada was spared the kind of prolonged drought that had parched the state and the West generally in the 1920s and 1930s. But as planners and meteorologists looked ahead to the last years of the twentieth century, there was much uncertainty about whether such success at water-witching could continue.[1]

For approximately a hundred years, Nevada law has provided for the distribution of water according to the principle of "prior appropriation," which holds that the first person to put a stream to "beneficial use" acquires a property right to the same amount of water so appropriated in all subsequent years, so long as the use continues. Water diverted from its natural streambed and put through a field or a mill on a continuing annual basis constitutes a property right that dates from the first recorded instance of such use. If there is a shortage in any particular year, the waters of the stream are not to be distributed among the users on the basis of need, nor is the shortage to be shared equally. Rather, the oldest rights must be honored first and fully in chronological order, if it is established that they have been beneficially and continuously used. The owners of the later water rights theoretically must make all the sacrifices—must see their fields parch and their cattle choke—in a dry year when there is not enough water for all.

The theory is clear enough, and it applies to underground water that may be pumped from wells in addition to stream flow. If rancher Smith's well is older in beneficial use than that of rancher Jones, and if the two wells begin to go dry, then Jones must stop pumping until Smith's needs—at least up to the amount that he appropriated at the earlier date—are met. Obviously the application of such a system in the dry valleys and canyons of Nevada and among the various "ditch companies" that own some of the oldest rights in the state is not easy. It is somewhat like herding wild cattle when water is in short supply, and there have been as many "water rustlers" as cattle thieves in that part of the country. In the dry years, the job of a water master—the individual appointed by the communities or the courts to supervise the distribution—is not an easy one.

By the mid-1940s, most of Nevada's rivers and streams had been appropriated to the full amount of their flows, or so it seemed; the rights of the users had more or less been defined by the courts and by tradition after two generations of litigation and practice. In the few cases still pending, the general outline of the settlements seemed rather clear, and most priority dates, rates of flow, and acre feet of annual entitlement were established. If population and technology had remained stable, Nevada might have had few water problems, but within a few years after mid-century, there were many more people seeking the bounty of the streams, drawing on the underground aquifers, seeding the clouds, and looking beyond the borders of the state for the precious elixir. The trouble was that everyone else in the West was doing the same thing, and the lawsuits proliferated.

A comprehensive study by the Mackay School of Mines of the University of Nevada and by the U.S. Geological Survey in 1964 made an important historical point. Before about 1914, Nevada's population centers, such as they were, were often determined by the locations of ore bodies, and water was a secondary consideration. More recently, the population centers have been concentrated around the perennial sources of water.[2]

It would be quite simple to manage the increasing demand on the limited water supplies if the doctrine of prior appropriation were the only rule for distribution, but it is not. While water law and distribution have traditionally been regarded as state, not federal, matters in the arid West, the federal government has certain recognized needs and rights. One of the most important is the so-called Winters Doctrine, enunciated by the U.S. Supreme Court in 1908, which holds that the United States had the right to reserve water for Indian reservations at the time they were established to accomplish the purposes for which they were created.[3] Any private appropriation of water after that date would be inferior. The government also had the right to claim water for other purposes prior to use, as in the case of the Newlands Project at Fernley and Fallon, which was established by the Newlands Reclamation Act of 1902.

The Truckee River Controversies

The Truckee River basin has been one of the historic testing grounds for the competing claims of water users relying upon the doctrine of prior appropriation and the U.S. government, which has at times represented the interests of the Newlands Project users and the Paiute Indians of the Pyramid Lake Indian Reservation. The 120-mile-long river, which originates on the California side of Lake Tahoe and empties into Pyramid Lake northeast of Reno, has one of the longest histories of intermittent water-rights controversies in the Far West, and, in the middle of the 1980s, the battles seemed far from over.

As early as 1870, an enterprising San Francisco engineer promoted the idea of diverting the waters of Lake Tahoe and the Truckee River westward through or across the Sierra Nevada to serve the Sacramento Valley and San Francisco. His scheme failed to win any significant support, so Nevadans were able to keep most of the Truckee's natural flow and to appropriate it to the valleys of the western part of the Great Basin.

In 1913, the federal government filed a "friendly lawsuit" to determine the amount of water due to the Pyramid Lake Indian Reservation and to claim much of the unappropriated water of the river for its Newlands Project, then under construction in the desert sixty miles east of Reno and Carson City. It was the first federal reclamation project of its kind, and the Department of the Interior made a claim to approximately half the average annual flow on the assumption that hundreds of thousands of acres of arid land could be cultivated with the excess water. This was the celebrated "Orr Ditch case," which turned out to be not so "friendly" after all, as it aroused farmers, utility companies, Lake Tahoe property owners, domestic water users, and others in the Truckee basin. It was still pending in 1940.

Most of the larger issues, however, seemed to be near settlement by that time, because a special master's proposed compromise had been in use for about fifteen years, and a Truckee River Agreement had been formulated in 1935 to which the U.S. government and most of the parties to the suit had consented. The U.S. District Court approved a final "consent" decree in 1944 and the case was apparently closed, because no one appealed.[4] It appeared that thirty years of arguments, testimony, engineering surveys, and scientific work had produced a permanent arrangement. When Lillard wrote his *Desert Challenge*, he believed that the Tahoe-Truckee water controversies were coming to an end.[5] But he, like "Pop" Squires, guessed wrong.

If we think of the Truckee River as a large plumbing system, the picture may become clearer. With the finalization of the Orr Ditch decree, it seemed that everyone on the system—the Lake Tahoe property owners, the utility company, the Truckee Meadows (Reno area) ranchers and farmers, the homeowners, the Truckee-Carson Irrigation District (TCID, or Newlands Project users), the federal government and its clients on the Pyramid Lake Paiute Reservation—understood how much water could be taken from the system at the various "faucets" and who had the earliest rights in times of shortage. The input to the system had been improved by the addition of a new reservoir at Boca on the Little Truckee in 1939; additional new storage units were added later. The Truckee-Carson district had a few dry years in the next three decades, but because the "plumbing" devices in the Orr Ditch settlement functioned smoothly, there was no serious trouble for a generation. Reno and its neighboring communities had plenty of water at very low rates and used it profusely to grow their lawns and sustain their trembling leaves.

In the 1970s, however, the whole system of ground rules began to collapse. The population growth in the Reno area started to outstrip the water supply available for municipal purposes in the drier years. The middle of the 1970s brought the most severe two-year drought since the 1930s. And to complicate matters further, in 1973 lawyers for the United States tried to reopen the Orr Ditch case on the ground that the Indians' interests had not been properly represented in the 1913–1944 lawsuit, because their right to a fishery had been overlooked. It was also asserted that there had been a conflict of interest, because in the earlier trial the government had represented both the Indians and the Newlands users. The federal government brought suit against 17,000 people who had actual or potential water rights along the river and requested more than half the average annual flow to maintain the lake.[6]

The new Truckee River suit was not unexpected. There had been a series of legal and administrative maneuvers in Washington earlier to try to force the TCID to yield some of its decreed water rights in favor of the Indians. The Fallon-Fernley region had doubled in population since 1940, and, as John Townley, the foremost historian of the Newlands Project experiment, said, the quarter-century from 1945 to 1970 was the period in which these communities matured; they were years of "relative prosperity and tranquility for residents of Churchill County and the Newlands Project."[7] Prices for farm output and hay were good, and it appeared that both Uncle Sam and the people who had invested in Newlands had helped fulfill the ancient prophecy about making the desert bloom. But then the Bureau of Reclamation, which for decades had not taken an active interest in how the TCID managed its waters, began to insist upon conservation measures that seemed harsh and unrealistic at the local level. In the meantime, the Pyramid Lake Paiutes, aided by federal fishery experts and a privately funded Native American rights organization, pressed for new litigation over the interpretation of the Winters Doctrine as it related to a fishery. All the other water users on the river named in the lawsuit were made defendants because the government's attorneys assumed that the entire flow of the river needed readjudication.

The case for the 17,000 defendants was built mainly on the judicial theory of *res judicata,* which holds that once a matter has been properly tried and a judgment rendered in the courts, it cannot be retried unless there is a showing of fraud or the discovery of new evidence that was not available at the time of the original trial. After another long and costly trial, Judge Blaine Anderson, a federal judge from Idaho who was designated to hear the matter, accepted this line of argument and ruled that the Orr Ditch case had properly litigated the issues. He therefore dismissed the suit and set the stage for the anticipated appeal. The issue then went to the Ninth Circuit Court of Appeals and ultimately to the U.S. Supreme Court.

In 1983, the Supreme Court affirmed Judge Anderson's ruling for the principle of *res judicata*. Thus the Orr Ditch matter seemed to be settled again, seventy years after it had been initiated.[8] However, the Paiutes then filed another case in a federal court in California, seeking the unappropriated water of Lake Tahoe and the upper Truckee west of the state line on the basis of the Winters Doctrine.

The Orr Ditch case is a prime example of how protracted and how complicated water controversies can be in the arid West. For a third of a century after the final principles of the Orr Ditch compromise had been agreed to by the parties in the 1930s, water users in the Truckee Basin had thought they had secure water rights and supplies. The drought and the change in U.S. water policies in the 1970s put that assumption to another severe test. The costs of maintaining Nevada's pioneering Newlands Reclamation Project had risen sharply, not only because of inflation but also because of the expense of litigation, which did not seem to end. In the meantime, the Indians were earnestly hoping that their fishery, together with more efficient use of irrigation water, would help the reservation Paiutes rise from their continuing level of poverty.

Another crucial dimension of the Truckee River situation was the condition of Lake Tahoe. All through the years when the Orr Ditch litigation and its sequel were underway, there was intermittent controversy over the use of the lands and waters around this magnificent alpine lake—one of the largest, deepest, and most beautiful of its kind in the world. The lake's natural splendor has been admired since the days when the young Mark Twain camped there in the 1860s, but a recent environmental historian correctly summarized, "Tahoe's scenic beauty has been its undoing."[9] Although the region had been stripped of much of its timber before the beginning of the twentieth century, its forests had gradually grown back and the basic ecological balance still survived at the beginning of the 1940s. Following the end of World War II, however, Tahoe became a tourist center; by the 1960s, ugly and destructive urban sprawl had been inflicted on its north and south shorelines. Because of erosion and pollution, the quality of its crystal-clear waters, like its other natural assets, deteriorated.

It was the tourist and gambling "industries," of course, that were most responsible for the transformation, as large resort casinos went into operation and lured customers and their automobiles by the tens of thousands. It was estimated that the population of the Tahoe basin during the busy months of July and August in 1948 had averaged about 27,000.[10] During the next thirty years, as boosters and gambling developers worked their will and the area became a year-round resort, the hordes came in increasing numbers. By 1980, the permanent population was estimated at 60,000 and the peak summer population, according to the U.S. Forest Service, was 223,000.[11]

Nevada and California have tried over the years to cooperate in planning for orderly growth and to preserve the purity of the water, but their efforts have been largely unsuccessful. They created, with the blessings of Congress, a California-Nevada Interstate Compact Commission to try to resolve water controversies on the Truckee, Carson, and Walker rivers. After thirteen years of negotiation, while the development continued apace, the two states reached agreement on all the important issues, including the sharing and management of Lake Tahoe's waters; by 1971, both state legislatures had ratified a compact. But Congress then balked at ratification of the compact, largely because of the protests of the Pyramid Lake Paiutes, who feared that its provisions would preclude their future chances to obtain more water. Thus the agreement that might have diminished the runaway growth was delayed.[12] In the meantime, commission members estimated that the population of the basin might eventually reach 400,000.[13]

In the early 1980s, the federal government was acquiring land to try to retard the more destructive commercial and urban developments, and the state of California approved a bond issue for $85 million to acquire environmentally threatened land in the Tahoe basin. Nevada, however, refused to join in this effort on a large scale.

In 1984, because of a legislative act, the Nevada voters were asked whether they would approve $20 million in bonds to make possible the purchase of environmentally sensitive land on the east side of the lake to prevent developments that would further damage the delicate natural balance. The voters statewide overwhelming rejected the bond issue; only those in Washoe County (the Reno area) favored the bond issue with a majority vote.

When Judge Anderson was hearing the evidence on the latest Truckee River case in 1975, government witnesses suggested that there might be enough underground water in the Reno-Sparks area to replace the amount that the government wanted for the reservation fishery and that increased pumping was feasible. The defense lawyers tried to show that this source was not sufficient to provide a long-term solution to the problem, but it did stir memories of past eras when underground aquifers had been extensively used in other desert areas.

The Las Vegas Valley and the Colorado River

Las Vegas, as a new frontier town from 1905 until 1940, seemed to be a prime example of a community that could function in a parched desert valley by pumping most of its water from underground. Almost from the town's beginning, the small natural spring that had served the original Mormon colony and the ranchers who followed had been supplemented by artesian wells and later by pumps, reaching ever deeper and further afield as the community grew. By 1939, there was an uncontrolled maze of pumping procedures and no systematic program for controlling and measuring the use of water. Some 450 different units were in operation, and many were wantonly careless in their use of water.

In that year, largely through the efforts of Alfred Merritt Smith, the state legislature enacted a law giving the state engineer the authority to regulate the pumping of underground water.[14] By that time it was clear to a few engineers that the Las Vegas Valley's underground sources were not being "recharged" as quickly as they were being pumped and that the long-range result would be the depletion of the crucial water table. It required several years for the state engineer's office to stop the unauthorized and often extravagant pumping.

In adopting the 1939 water law, Nevada became a leader among the far western states in the control and management of its underground water resources. It was, for example, ahead of California, where the lack of adequate regulation allowed the damage to some aquifers to continue much longer. Largely in response to the new Nevada policy, the Las Vegas area began to develop a rational program designed to encourage long-range water management.[15] It was common in the 1940s for Las Vegans to use an average of 600 gallons of water per person per day during the summer to irrigate their lawns and to keep their homes cool. Yet they paid only two dollars per month for an unlimited supply.[16] The level of the aquifer was falling so rapidly that some natural plants had died by the time the conservation measures became effective. Las Vegas seemed to be in danger of going the way of some oases on the edge of the African Sahara, where excessive use of a limited supply of water had ended with the destruction of the source itself—and the strangling of the oasis by the desert.

In the case of Las Vegas, however, there was a solution less than twenty miles away in the Colorado River. In 1922, the several western states that had some claim to the river had signed the Colorado River Compact, dividing its waters among them. Nevada had been granted 300,000 acre feet per year, or about 2 percent of the estimated average annual flow. The Compact had allowed 7.5 million acre feet (m.a.f.) to the "upper basin" states, and an equal amount to the "lower basin" states; the latter included Nevada, Arizona, and California. The compact provided that California could have 4.2 m.a.f. and Arizona 2.8 m.a.f. Nevada's .3 m.a.f. may seem to be only a trickle in terms of the total river flow, but in the 1920s, and even in 1940, it seemed a bonus for the driest state.

This distribution meant little until the building of Hoover Dam in the early 1930s and the filling of Lake Mead behind it. By 1941, however, there was a vast reservoir and an abundance of cheap power from the dam's hydroelectric plant, and when the government faced its desperate wartime need for a magnesium processing plant, it made sense to transport water and power into the Las Vegas Valley and to build the plant there. Thus, in 1942, the government financed the pumping of the first Colorado River water across the mountains into the Las Vegas Valley to facilitate the operation of the Basic Magnesium Plant. After the initial phase of construction and magnesium production had been completed, the valley had an extra 20,000 acre feet per year, which supplemented its ground water supply adequately until the 1960s, in spite of the fact that there were a number of dry years in the interval.[17]

Thus much of the early growth of Las Vegas was lubricated by the bonus water that the government had provided for a wartime enterprise.

This reprieve gave the Las Vegas Valley time to reorganize its water distribution system and to replace the poorly managed Las Vegas Land and Water Company, which had been created in 1905, with a valley-wide authority. It also provided the leisure to plan the second and third phases of a system to transport the remainder of the state's 300,000 m.a.f. per year from Lake Mead to the Las Vegas Valley. The first large transfusion came in 1971, and the final stage was completed a decade later.

Before the second and third phases had been started, however, there had been another long, costly interstate struggle over the rights to the flow of the river. In 1952, Arizona filed suit against California, claiming that its share was too small and California's too large. Nevada intervened in the suit in order to protect its rights, and following the prompting of Senator George W. Malone, a former state engineer and an ardent advocate of the "Nevada first" attitude, the state's lawyers made a claim for 800,000 acre feet rather than 300,000. This was typical of the western approach to water rights; the theory was that one must claim at least twice as much as one is entitled to in order to get a fair share. This effort failed—or perhaps it succeeded, depending on one's point of view—and when the Supreme Court ruling came in 1963, Nevada was left with its original 300,000 acre feet of annual flow, a result that in the circumstances was treated as a victory.[18]

Yet that chronic dark cloud—the fear of drought—did not disappear with the "victory" of 1963. Written into the *Arizona* v. *California* decree was a provision that in a dry year it might be necessary to reduce the amount of water to all users under a formula to be devised by the Department of the Interior. Those who knew the Colorado River best at the beginning of the 1980s warned that the calculated 7.5 m.a.f. annual flow for the lower basin was too high; there had not been that much water in the main channel on the average over the past fifty years. A crisis was avoided because most of the potential water users, including Nevada, were unable to use all of their decreed rights, and the huge Central Arizona Project was less than half finished. It was estimated that when the latter system did begin to take new, large-volume flows eastward toward Phoenix and Tucson, the vast plumbing system would be severely tested. Nature, often capricious in such matters, granted another reprieve in the middle 1980s, sending more snow and rain and dumping more water into the basin in 1982–1984 than at any time in the previous half-century. The reservoirs behind Hoover Dam and the other large dams on the river were full in 1984, and, like the pharaohs of Egypt, the water users of the Southwest were not disposed to worry about famine in a season of plenty.

As of 1980, Nevada was using only about one-third of its 300,000 acre feet, but it was preparing to divert most of it into the Las Vegas Valley within the next few years. Several years earlier, the state engineer's office had commissioned a long-range projection of the future needs of the Las Vegas basin, and it calculated that, by the year 2020, there would be between 1.1 and 1.3 million people in the metropolitan area. In that case, the region would need between 28 and 39 percent more water forty years hence than was then available from the underground sources, from Lake Mead, and from the reclaiming of waste water. Las Vegas seemed to have a choice of limiting its own growth or of finding still more sources of water from outside the valley to accommodate the future developments. Among the ideas offered for consideration was the transfer of water from the Pahranagat Valley (90 miles north) or Railroad Valley (175 miles north) or from outside the state.[19]

All too often in the West, water has been diverted to where the money is, so it was conceivable that within the next twenty years or so, Las Vegas could be reaching northward into central Nevada, or into Utah or Idaho, in the same way that Los Angeles reached northward into the Sierra Nevada and central California in the early twentieth century. The difficulty, of course, is that northern and central Nevada and the neighboring states do not have any obvious sources of surplus water to spare. In any case, it would be an odd variation on the historical pattern of geopolitical plumbing in the Far West to transfer water *into* the Colorado basin.

New Approaches for the 1980s

Before the 1980s, it was the pattern of those who relied upon the Colorado River—like those who depended upon the Truckee, Carson, and other western Nevada streams—to fight in the courts over the flow. The judicial branch has been the great referee, and the process has been costly to all users. Given the impending shortage that is likely to occur in any extended dry spell, it seems certain that the long, tedious chain of litigation will continue into the final decade of the twentieth century, unless a new spirit of cooperation, a change in the pattern of growth, a new source of water, or some combination of these is found.

There may be a new tendency toward cooperation within the Colorado River basin, as there has been in the Tahoe basin, in view of the growing recognition that the supply of water is finite and now overcommitted. As Philip Fradkin has written:

> The river's waters and the land surrounding it in the basin—the heartland of the West—are fused together in a common destiny, as are those areas outside the watershed to which Colorado River water is diverted—southern California, Salt Lake valley, Colorado's Front Range, and the Rio Grande valley in New Mexico. . . . Not the Rocky Mountains nor the Pacific Ocean, but the Colorado River which flows from one toward the other, is the single most unifying geographical and political factor in the West. The river has been the most significant catalyst in the politics of the West since the turn of the century.[20]

Yet the Colorado River basin has provided one of the best historical examples of how difficult it is to reconcile the conflicting water-law principles and to make them adaptable to changing needs. The Colorado flows through seven states and into Mexico, which also has treaty rights to a portion of the flow. The states, the seventy-odd counties, and the thirty Indian tribes with their Winters Doctrine reserved rights all have claims.[21] Nevada and Las Vegas are only two of more than a hundred jurisdictions that stand along the river bank like choking oxen, pawing for a slightly larger mud-hole from which to drink.

As the search for new sources of water intensified in the 1970s, the Las Vegas Valley Water District sought the help of a branch of the University of Nevada—the Water Resources Center of the Desert Research Institute. Since 1959, this agency has been developing data on the quality and quantity of Nevada's waters, and in the past two decades its scientists have produced hundreds of technical studies, which may possibly point toward a solution of the problems that could be foreseen in the early 1980s.

The DRI scientists have been engaged in a sophisticated form of "water-witching." Of the many research projects that have been undertaken, the one that generated most interest at the beginning of the 1980s was a plan to probe the very deep levels of carbonate rock that underlie most of southern and eastern Nevada and part of western Utah. Beneath most of Clark, Lincoln, and White Pine counties and parts of Elko, Eureka, and Nye are massive layers of such rock.[22] There had been almost no deep drilling of these layers as of 1983, but evidence from caves, mines, wildcat oil and gas wells, and springs led scientists to hypothesize that there might be water in such quantity that it would solve the problem of a desert economy for generations.

The scientific data had not yet confirmed the hypothesis in the early 1980s, but preliminary indications were tantalizing. When the U.S. Air Force proposed to construct 4,600 missile sites for the MX system in the desert valleys of Nevada and Utah, it chose almost exactly the same area under which the carbonate strata lie—a fact that startled and worried Nevada's water use planners. During the discussions between the Air Force designers, the representatives of the Nevada state engineer's office, and the Desert Research Institute hydrologists in 1980 and 1981, the Air Force announced its willingness to finance the drilling of the wells that would be necessary to test the deep aquifers and to determine their relationship to the subsurface ground water at the higher levels. One such well was drilled near Coyote Springs in Clark County, and it produced a good flow. But in October, 1981, when President Ronald Reagan disapproved of the basing mode that would have spread the missiles over some 40,000 square miles, the deep-aquifer drilling ceased.

The basic question remained: Did there exist, two or three miles beneath the arid surface, large caverns like those at Lehman Caves, either filled with water or capable of receiving it from the surrounding rock? Was that water pure, and could it be raised to the surface cheaply enough to supply the needs of a thirsty commonwealth?

Although much information had been developed, the relationship between the deep aquifers and the waters nearer the surface continued to be unknown. It may require a dozen deep wells, costing a million dollars or more each, to learn whether sufficient quantities can be raised to justify the cost without, at the same time, draining the surface and artesian waters on which existing rights are based. In short, the quest became three-dimensional, involving not only the appropriation of waters along and immediately beneath the surface, but far deeper into the earth than Nevada's eager miners ever dreamed of going in their quest for precious metals.

Even if there is a sea of available pure water in the carbonate aquifers—and there are skeptics who doubt it—it cannot be assumed that this will solve the problems of the northern and western parts of the state. Beneath the fully committed and overcommitted watersheds of the Carson, Truckee, Walker, and Humboldt rivers, there are no known carbonate aquifers. If there is a solution to the water shortages of those regions, could it be in the clouds, rather than underground?

In the rural counties, there has long been interest in and controversy over the possibility of building reservoirs to catch more of the winter and spring runoff from the mountains for beneficial use in the closed basins of the regions. The Rye Patch Reservoir of the lower Humboldt Valley and Weber Reservoir on the Walker River Indian Reservation, both built in the middle 1930s, would seem to testify to the benefit that downstream users can receive from such installations, and similar dams have been built in recent years in a dozen other places in Nevada. But such dams occasionally disturb existing water rights, and a number of projects proposed by the U.S. Army Corps of Engineers or Bureau of Reclamation officials did not receive enough local support to be translated into political pressure and funding. Proposals for dams on the north and south forks of the Humboldt and on Mary's River provoked opposition because downstream users worried about the long-range effects on the quality and quantity of their supplies.[23] Likewise, on the Carson River, much suspicion developed over the Bureau of Reclamation's proposal in the 1956 Washoe Project to build the Watasheamu Reservoir on the east fork of the Carson River. Yet the Carson basin by the early 1980s had experienced a population growth that ran far ahead of the available water supply and the state government had imposed a moratorium on new residential construction in Carson City because there was no more water to distribute. In 1982, a task force recommended the construction of the Watasheamu Reservoir and yet another facility—called the Comstock Dam—below Carson City to make it possible to impound more of the occasional floodwaters.[24]

New reservoirs would be useless, of course, without the water to fill them. Another significant thrust of the Desert Research Institute's research in the 1970s was its weather modification studies—cloud-seeding experiments to ascertain whether more rain could be brought down from the clouds as they pass over the watersheds. In 1970, a team of DRI scientists headed by Professor Joseph Warburton initiated the Pyramid Lake Pilot Project, a five-year program to test the possibilities for seeding clouds at opportune times in the upper Truckee River basin. While the inquiry left many questions without definitive answers, there were preliminary indications that the seeding had produced 25 percent more precipitation than would normally be expected.[25] Translated into snowpack on the slopes, this meant a substantial increase in the number of acre feet of water for the Truckee River and Pyramid Lake.

During the drought that afflicted the Far West in the winter seasons of 1975–1976 and 1976–1977, the Nevada legislature asked the DRI to undertake an emergency cloud-seeding program. In response to this call, the scientists selected five areas—Tahoe-Truckee, Walker River, Spring Mountain west of Las Vegas, and Ely and Elko—for systematic seeding. Again, while the results could not be called definitive, preliminary interpretations of the evidence were encouraging.[26]

It was too early to tell in the mid-1980s whether this kind of experimentation would produce strategies that would ease Nevada's chronic water problems. Scientific verification of the hypotheses in such matters requires much time and financing, and certain risks had to be evaluated. The DRI scientists were cautious not to experiment with storms when a danger of flooding or of avalanche seemed to be present, and they avoided experiments when there was a probability that the precipitation would complicate heavy highway traffic flow. Such considerations obviously delayed their investigations. Like all important scientific enterprises, this one had to be checked against the evidence produced by similar cloud-seeding experiments elsewhere.

It also seems certain that some form of interstate cooperation will be essential as rain-making becomes more common and as the state of the art improves, because the need for more water is now recognized as a regional, not merely a state, problem. It will not be surprising if the federal government undertakes regulatory responsibilities in this field. Certainly the role of Washington in the distribution of water within a state's borders has been increasing, and the doctrine of federal reserved rights, initially enunciated in the Winters case as it applied to Indian reservations, has come to have broader applications. A notable 1976 U.S. Supreme Court case involving Nevada, often called the Devil's Hole or "pupfish" case, established that the federal government has the right to reserve waters for the preservation of an endangered species of wildlife when it has set aside an area for that purpose.[27] Thus each time the United States reclassifies part of the public domain for a specific purpose, it may be presumed to have taken a sufficient amount of unappropriated water. This doctrine holds much potential for increased federal control of water if and when new sources are discovered.

The controversy over the MX racetrack missile system in 1980–1981 led to one potentially important development in water management policy. The federal government, which for many years had taken the position that it had no obligation to file for water rights with the state engineer's office when it wanted water for a specific purpose, yielded the point and agreed to follow state procedures. The U.S. Air Force obviously took this step in order to reduce the local fears that the MX development would dry up existing sources or disturb legally established rights. By the summer of 1981, the Air Force had filed

hundreds of applications with the state engineer, but when President
Reagan announced his decision to dispense with the racetrack system,
the applications were suspended, and they were ultimately withdrawn in
the summer of 1983. The possibility remained, however, that some
other federal agency could file such claims on virtually all of the
remaining water in Nevada—or any other state. The Bureau of Land
Management had already made a claim to all springs and water holes on
the public domain from which water had not been appropriated. Litigation was anticipated over the legality of that claim.

A "New" Strategy: Conservation

One of the most obvious approaches to Nevada's water problem
received little serious attention until the 1970s—a systematic policy of
conservation. The widespread waste of water in many parts of the state
had become a matter of increasing concern. Alfred Merritt Smith, that
prophetic voice fom an earlier era, had told a conference as early as 1949
that more than half the water designated for irrigation and domestic
purposes in the state was being wasted, and there was no serious
challenge to his estimate, nor was there any meaningful response from
the public or politicians.

In the late 1970s, the Nevada Division of Water Planning took up the
task of encouraging more responsible use of the resources available.[28]
Planning Administrator James P. Hawke estimated on the basis of a
comprehensive survey that water demands could be reduced by 10
percent by the implementation of elementary conservation measures,
primarily the modification of irrigation, landscaping, and household
practices.

As of the mid-1980s, residents of Reno still did not have water meters
to measure the amount of usage and to impose charges on the basis of
consumption; state laws written when the city was much smaller still
operated. During the dry years of the mid-1970s, Reno residents were
asked to conserve water in their homes and gardens to assure an adequate
supply for the following year, but almost simultaneously the City
Council approved the construction of additional hotel-casinos to
accommodate more tourists. The request for conservation apparently
backfired, as a number of residents wrote letters to the editors of the
local newspapers, refusing to conserve as long as the local governments
were allowing commercial expansion—especially in the gambling sec-
tor—to continue virtually uncontrolled.

Since the 1930s, the primary responsibility for administering the state's water laws has rested with the state engineer, but a study made by the legislative commission in 1979–1980 found that office to be understaffed, its record-keeping system inadequate, and the salaries paid to its hydraulic engineers too low to attract and retain competent professional experts.[29] A recommendation that several new positions be added to the division of water resources won approval in the 1981 legislature, but when Governor Robert List ordered a budget cut due to a revenue shortfall in 1982, many of these positions were lost.

A panoramic survey of the history of water use, management, litigation, and research in the Sagebrush State from the 1940s to the 1980s showed that the water managers—in the state engineer's office, the Department of Conservation and Natural Resources, the Division of Water Planning, and the water masters—had done remarkably well in anticipating problems. The legal profession deserved good marks, on the whole, for litigating complex issues in the courts to the benefit of most people directly involved. Legislation was generally adequate, and the state had received better scientific and technical research through its universities than it was willing to pay for; the federal government's grants financed much of the water research and development. The legislature has traditionally been stingy in its support for any kind of research, and, if this attitude continues, the chances for long-term solutions that could serve for another forty years are remote indeed.

As of the summer of 1984, the reservoirs and lakes were full as a result of two wet winters in sequence. Even the Humboldt Sink, the low-lying basin that receives the last waters of the modest little "river" of that name, looked deceptively like a legitimate lake and was spilling its excess waters into the Carson Sink for the first time in a half-century. Pyramid Lake was the highest it had been in more than thirty years; water was gushing through the spillways at Hoover Dam for the first time since it was built; and the grazing cattle found their evening drinks in places where no water had been in that season in their lifetime. Highways had been flooded here and there, old bridges became untrustworthy, and traditional quarrels about water rights and concerns about shortages went into limbo. The year 1984 was clearly not a time to worry about water, and there was no Alfred Merritt Smith on hand to remind Nevadans that there might be a future to consider.

CHAPTER 4

THE LAND AND ITS USES

OUT IN THE RUGGED mountain ranges of Nevada, it is possible to forget, for a while, the transformations that have occurred in the valleys in the extreme southern and western corners of the state. The hiker or hunter who flees from the urban confusion to imbibe the silences and the aroma of the sage and juniper could do it almost as well in the 1980s as in the 1940s, if the urge to escape were strong enough. Yet there was a profound change, not so much in the land itself, because much of it was still truly wilderness, but in the prevailing attitudes toward the land in Washington, Las Vegas, and Carson City. It was evident by 1980 that the "wide open spaces" so frequently celebrated by people who, fortunately, seldom cast their shadows there are in danger of being exploited recklessly, just as the water supplies have been.

Most of the valleys in which water is available have been tamed, fenced, improved for grazing, subdivided, or otherwise claimed, but the mountains that surround them—and all of Nevada's valleys are framed or circled by mountain barriers—have suffered little alteration since the days of the mining booms of old. It is the mountain ranges, most of them widely separated by the broad valleys stretching generally in a north-south direction, that have given Nevada its topographical distinction, and these rugged uplands still stand essentially defiant of human enterprise. Some are scarred here and there by the work of long-dead prospectors; most of them yielded very little for the labor bestowed upon them. More than half of them are treeless and lacking water, but every Nevadan whose horizons extend beyond the city limits has a favorite mountain, a place of pilgrimage in fact or in imagination, a spiritual reference point near at hand.

The Nevada desert does not readily yield to prose description, partly because there is so much subtle variety in it. In his recent book *Basin and Range,* John McPhee produced one of the most appealing images of recent times:

> Each range here is like a warship standing on its own, the Great Basin is an ocean of loose sediment with these mountains standing in it as if they were members of a fleet without precedent, assembled at Guam to assault Japan.[1]

It requires an ambitious metaphor to describe this land, and McPhee's reminds us of how easily we have come to think in terms of warfare and aggression in these latter days of the twentieth century. A half-century ago, perhaps, we would have been disposed to contemplate our landscape in more gentle images. Are not the ranges more like a disorganized flotilla of variegated vessels, some of them tall ships at full sail, moving majestically northward in a strong wind, accompanied by a disorderly assortment of smaller craft—dinghies, rafts, and tubs—some straying, some listing as though their inebriated captains had no regard for the general plans of the fleet? Yet McPhee's metaphor is undoubtedly more appropriate for our time, because Nevada's land has increasingly been treated as a real or potential federal preserve, useful mainly for military activities and nuclear experimentation, and both the mountains and the valleys have become a jurisdictional battleground.

For the first hundred years of statehood, Nevadans generally had little objection to the land policies they had inherited at the time of the state's admission to the Union. Before the 1970s, there were no serious challenges to the fact that, of the 70.7 million acres of land within the state's borders, about 60 million had some measure of federal administration or ownership, and another million acres had been set aside for Indian reservations. Only about 9.5 million acres were in private ownership, and the railroads had much of that, because Congress had made vast land grants in the middle of the nineteenth century to stimulate construction of the transcontinental lines. The state government owned only a tiny fragment of the land within its borders.

The fact that the federal government held the land had caused little concern since the 1860s, because most of it had been open for the use of miners and cattlemen. One could stake an unpatented mining claim according to the traditional frontier procedures and thus gain title to the mineral rights at no cost, and, if there were sufficient incentive, one could have the claim surveyed and get a fee patent title. And the cattleman or sheep herder could run his animals on the open range at nominal cost and, until the 1930s, with little regulation. This led to overgrazing, and in 1934 the federal government began to ration range rights under the Taylor Grazing Act. By the 1970s, the regulations had become a tangled mass of decrees, hated by the ranchers and miners.

Of the 60 million acres under federal control, about 80 percent was unappropriated public domain, which had never been designated for any specific national use and thus was basically open for mining, livestock grazing, and recreation. Congress had at various times set aside 5 million acres as national forests, and in the 1940s it withdrew more than 3 million acres for national defense needs—for the Las Vegas Bombing and Gunnery Range, for example. Such withdrawals caused no particular concern. It was still possible at mid-century for a private citizen to obtain land under the Homestead Act or the Desert Land Act; although there were administrative hurdles, the venerable federal policy of land distribution to industrious yeomen who would "prove up on it" was still intact in the law books.

A New Land Policy

In 1966, Congress created a Public Land Law Review Commission to study the whole question of public land policy and to make recommendations for new management policies for the public domain. The law established a commission of nineteen persons, and Nevada's interests were well represented; both Senator Alan Bible and Congressman Walter S. Baring were members. In addition, two Nevadans sat on the small advisory council that assisted the commission—John Marvel, a Battle Mountain rancher, and W. Howard Gray, who was chairman of the Public Lands Committee of the American Mining Congress. When the commission issued its report in June, 1970, it proposed fundamental changes in the policy of the U.S. government toward the unappropriated public lands.[2]

The commission decided that there were many archaic features in the existing land policy. No one could legitimately assert that its implications were hidden; the main bombshell appeared on the first page:

We . . . recommend that:
The policy of large-scale disposal of public lands reflected by the majority of statutes in force today be revised and that future disposal should be only

of those lands that will achieve maximum benefit for the general public in non-Federal ownership, while retaining in Federal ownership those whose values must be preserved so that they may be used and enjoyed by all Americans.[3]

This should have been a signal, if one were needed, to the western states that the long-standing federal policies on which their people had relied, including the assumption that they were entitled to virtually unsupervised use of the land, were undergoing a fundamental change. The additional recommendations underscored a trend toward increased planning and management from Washington. They included:

(1) a proposal for more systematic planning to achieve "the maximum number of compatible uses";

(2) a proposal that new "Federal statutory guidelines," enforced by federal licensing power, be put in place to assure the protection of a deteriorating natural environment;

(3) a proposal that guidelines be established to provide that "the United States receive full value for the use of the public lands and their resources . . .";

(4) several proposals designed to meet the needs and interests of the traditional users of the public lands, such as the cattlemen, the mining associations, and communities seeking blocks of land for expansion, and payments in lieu of taxes from the federal to local governments, and the reduction of bureaucratic red tape at the national level.[4]

It was undoubtedly the latter recommendations that made the whole package palatable to Nevada interests, insofar as they were aware of them, in 1970. There was no active interest in the report in the state at that point; the reaction to its implications came like a time-delayed bomb several years later, after the basic principles of the commission's findings had been enacted into law.

The Sagebrush Rebellion

Congress passed the Federal Land Policy and Management Act (FLPMA) in 1976, which declared at the outset "it is the Policy of the United States that . . . the public lands be retained in Federal ownership, unless as a result of land use planning procedure provided for in this Act, it is determined that disposal of a particular parcel will serve the national interest. . . ."[5]

The passage of this law, coupled with the growing resentment within Nevada toward the Bureau of Land Management, lighted the fuse to the

Sagebrush Rebellion in Elko County. There some cattlemen, convinced that their range rights were in jeopardy, took the initiative in designing and promoting state legislation that challenged the authority of the federal government to control and manage the public domain on a permanent basis. In their view, the solution to the rangeland problems was not more management from Washington, but more local control. Dean Rhoads, an Elko livestock owner and a member of the State Assembly, became the leading sponsor of the bill—enacted into law in the 1979 session of the legislature—which claimed that the public domain was the property of the state of Nevada.[6]

The reasoning behind the Sagebrush Rebellion was based upon historical claims and attitudes that were as old as the state itself. Nevada had been admitted to the Union in 1864 with some federal land grant entitlements that it could not effectively use, because the land distribution system designed for the Middle West soon after the American Revolution did not work well in Nevada's arid mountains and valleys. It was not easy, for example, to take 40, or 320, or 640 acres laid out in a square according to lines of latitude and longitude and make it productive in the alkaline basins of the West. Nevada had been entitled to receive, for school purposes, the 16th and 36th sections of each township—a right that was valuable for a state like Illinois where virtually every township had rich soil, but almost useless in Nevada's Forty-Mile Desert. So Nevada had, in 1880, surrendered a 3.9-million-acre grant for school lands to the federal government in exchange for the right to select about 2.0 million acres in those places where the land could best be used—or at least where the chance of selling it was best.

In addition, the men who wrote Nevada's 1864 Constitution had been required by Congress to insert a section in the state's fundamental law to the effect that the people of Nevada "forever disclaim all right and title to the unappropriated public lands lying within said territory [i.e., Nevada], and the same shall be and remain at the sole and entire disposition of the United States. . . ."[7] Nevada was the first western state to be forced to adopt such a disclaimer, and this provision—coupled with the 1880 land swap—apparently placed the state in a perpetually inferior position to the federal government and to most other states when it sought to obtain more lands for its own uses and for its citizens and when it tried to set land-use policies within its borders. Nevada had received land grants that were proportionally much smaller than those of its neighbors; Utah, Arizona, and New Mexico had each received about 11 percent of their total areas in federal land grants, while Nevada had received less than 4 percent.

The authors of the Sagebrush Rebellion took the position that the "disclaimer clause" in the Nevada Constitution was invalid because it had been forced upon the state as a condition of its admission to the Union. They argued that in some counties, particularly in the mining region, federal holdings constituted as much as 97 percent of the total area. Jurisdiction over the public domain was divided among 17 different federal agencies, many of which were not readily accessible or sympathetic to local needs and interests. The state and counties derived little or no tax revenue from federal lands, and some federal practices, such as weapons testing, had reduced the future usefulness of vast areas. So proponents of the rebellion argued in enacting their statute and preparing their legal case in Carson City.

There was another line of reasoning that raised yet another constitutional issue. Since the founding of the American Republic, the courts had accepted the principle that all states had been admitted to the Union on an "equal footing," and that each had a measure of sovereignty. The sagebrush rebels argued that Nevada had in effect been denied its "equal footing" and its proper share of state sovereignty because it had not been allowed to exercise a reasonable amount of jurisdiction over the land within its own borders. And the 1979 legislature—not easily persuaded to spend money for social or educational needs—appropriated $250,000 to test this theory in the courts. The vote in both houses was overwhelmingly favorable.

The Sagebrush Rebellion received early attention and nominal—but not much financial—support in other western states where there were large areas of the public domain. The national news media, with typical hyperbole, represented the rebellion as one of the most serious challenges to federal authority since the Civil War. *Newsweek* described an attitude of defiance to national authority spreading across the "Angry West," and featured the Nevada dimensions of the donnybrook.[8]

Not all Nevadans rallied to the banners of the rebellion. Some conservationists expressed the fear that Nevada was poorly prepared to assume the burdens and responsibilities of administering more than 40 million acres of the public domain, if it should receive title to it. The historical record showed that when Nevada had received its early land grants, it had managed them badly; there was a record of corruption when the early officers of the state had been in the business of distributing the acreages that had been available for educational and other purposes. State Senator Clifton Young of Reno, one of the few members of the legislature to vote and speak against the rebellion concept, described the movement as a "combination of demagoguery, avarice, and animosity and a handy way of venting spleen against the hated Feds."[9]

The tactical problem for lawyers from the Nevada Attorney General's Office was to find a forum and a legal strategy for taking the rebellion into the federal courts. Since the U.S. government cannot be sued without its consent, and since it seemed unlikely that Congress or the federal agencies would consent to direct litigation on an issue of this kind, Nevada lawyers tried unsuccessfully to find a way of getting the matter to trial on the precise issues they had in mind.

In the meantime, the election of Ronald Reagan as president in 1980 gave some hope to the originators of the rebellion, because he was thought to be sympathetic to their interests. During his presidential campaign, he had praised the rebellion and had deplored excessive federal regulation of the public lands. But when his first secretary of the interior, James Watt, went to the opposite extreme and proposed selling many federal properties—including the sale of much of the public domain—it brought new alarums.[10] This suggestion, which obviously was categorically opposed to the principles of FLPMA, got little support from the livestock interests, because it was unclear what would happen to their grazing privileges if the land were sold.

Nevada's livestock interests found themselves "in the middle" in the great land debate. Neither increased federal regulation of the ranges nor a large-scale "sell-off" seemed satisfactory. On the other hand, they had not yet convinced their fellow Nevadans or interested out-of-state groups that the state itself had the means of taking over the burden of managing the lands responsibly. In addition, Nevada cattlemen had a reputation, which may or may not have been deserved, of abusing the rangelands by putting more livestock on the public domain than BLM regulations allowed. Philip Fradkin in his travels through the West came to this conclusion:

> The Great Basin in Nevada is a closed-off society that tends to do as it pleases, regardless of what the federal government says. There is more illegal grazing on public lands, politely termed trespassing, in Nevada than in any other state.[11]

This would be difficult to prove, but few Nevadans in the cattle country would deny, in casual conversation, that there were ways around the regulators from Washington. Many would acknowledge that the quality of the range had deteriorated in the previous quarter-century.

In the Humboldt Valley, where the Sagebrush Rebellion was born and where the state's most productive livestock enterprises have operated over the decades, the controversies over the public lands and the waters are closely connected, because the ranges will sustain the livestock only so long as streams and springs are available. The Division of Water Planning in Carson City counted more than 1,200 streams in the state, and about 700 of them are within or north of the Humboldt basin. If federal control were extended to them, it was feared, the cattle and sheep businesses would be strangled by regulation.

From the viewpoint of the federal agencies that have responsibility for administering the land and protecting its resources, the problem is no less complex; Nevada has not been an easy client with which to deal. The Bureau of Land Management, created in 1946 by the consolidation of earlier agencies, has a mandate from Congress and its parent office, the Department of the Interior, to conserve the dwindling resources of the public domain. It has jurisdiction over 457 million acres of public land—more than half of it in Alaska and about a tenth of it in Nevada. From its point of view, the federal government's role has changed from a policy of "disposal," which lasted from the earliest days of the Republic until about 1934, to "custodial management" from 1934 to about 1950, and to "intensive management" since about 1950.[12] From this perspective, FLPMA was a logical and necessary step in the evolution of a national land policy. It was "an accurate mirror of shifting public attitudes about public lands." Because the Congress had enacted such laws as the National Environmental Policy Act, the Clean Air Act, various water pollution control laws, the Endangered Species Act, and others, the region that had once been "virtually the sole preserve of western livestock operators and mining interests" had become a center of national interest. The public lands constituted the "nation's resource storehouse," containing most of the United States' known oil and coal reserves, natural gas, geothermal possibilities, and the best forestry and wildlife resources.[13]

At the beginning of 1980, the Forest Service of the U.S. Department of Agriculture—which shares responsibility for grazing land management—published a 650-page study of the forest and range situation in the United States.[14] Taking into account the growth of population in the past half-century and the rising incomes of the population, it showed that consumption of forest and range products was increasing rapidly, and it estimated that demand for these products would soon exceed the supplies. Even though the nation has a vast forest/range/water resource, this has not been managed to achieve the best possible results, and the demands upon it are escalating. This study produced additional arguments for more careful planning and substantial investment in the renewable natural resources, including fish, wildlife, grazing, and timber and water conservation.

Such a vast planning and management exercise as the one proposed here has much in common with FLPMA, and if it were undertaken in Nevada in conjunction with other states, it would certainly meet resistance. Whether the attitude that spawned the Sagebrush Rebellion could ever be reconciled with the obvious need for more careful utilization of the resources of the region was an open question. Nevada's pride in its local prerogatives was so intense that it left little room for any kind of reconciliation with other jurisdictions.

Robert Burford (director of the BLM under President Reagan and Secretary of the Interior Watt) wrote in 1982:

> In this Administration, we are going to be decision makers. That's what we were called in to do—and that's what we'll do. We may make some people unhappy because we do make decisions rather than endlessly analyze or study. However, we have two guiding precepts: economic recovery and the national interest. We think these precepts will guide us well in producing results.[15]

In Nevada, that could be taken as a reassuring offer of peace, a declaration of war, or merely more political rhetoric. The jury was still out in the mid-1980s, because no one in Washington or Nevada had a more satisfactory land policy—at least not one that they were willing to risk their political scalps for—than the one that had been in effect for nearly a half-century.

The MX Controversy

In the same month that the Sagebrush Rebellion bill became law in Nevada—June, 1979—another decision about Great Basin lands was made across the continent in Washington, and the announcement of this new idea ultimately made the action of the Nevada legislature and the subsequent legal maneuvering on the rebellion look like a kindergarten game. This decision, announced by President Jimmy Carter, anticipated the building of 4,600 missile launching sites to be scattered across the Nevada and Utah deserts, capable of storing and firing the so-called Missile-Experimental, or MX. It was by far the largest and most expensive military enterprise ever conceived; it anticipated the storing and occasional shuttling of 200 massive nuclear weapons among the missile sites to prepare for a possible attack against a potential enemy halfway around the world.

The MX scheme was the brainchild of U.S. Air Force strategists in the Pentagon, who had become hypnotized by the arms race between the United States and the Soviet Union and who had assumed that the only means of deterring a nuclear attack on the United States was to build an ever-larger arsenal in this country. As proposed, the deployment zone would have encompassed an area as large as the state of Pennsylvania in central and south-central Nevada and southwestern Utah. The Air Force strategists had become convinced that the existing Inter-Continental Ballistics Missile system—with hundreds of missiles stored in silos in the Rocky Mountains and Middle West—was vulnerable to first-strike destruction in the event of an enemy attack. For several months after the MX decision was announced, most of the Nevada citizenry seemed stoical and unconcerned, partly because well-prepared Air Force spokesmen and news releases assured that there would be little disruption of the land or life-style of the residents in the deployment area. And the Pentagon spokesmen appealed, quite effectively at first, to the state's long-standing willingness to support any national defense measures.

The Air Force assurances included not only newspaper and television publicity but also "scoping meetings," which took the Pentagon's representatives into the remote towns of the central Great Basin as well as into Reno, Las Vegas, and Salt Lake City. The promises to the local populace were simple and often repeated. Well-designed exhibits and slide shows made the case for the impending Soviet menace, promised large dollar investments for the "impacted area," and proceeded to a soothing assurance that there would be little or no harmful effect on the Nevada and Utah landscape. One pamphlet said:

> Preserving the quality of the environment is a paramount Air Force concern. Specifically the M-X system is being designed to minimize adverse effects on the environment. Water and other resources needed by the system will be conserved in strict accordance with state laws. This will insure the system will be able to coexist with wildlife, mining, ranching and recreation. Each of the 4,600 shelters will be fenced unobtrusively on a two and one-half acre site. . . . For M-X the total amount of fenced land closed to the public will be about 25 nautical miles (a little less than 21,200 acres).[16]

At first the local opposition was confined to a small number of pacifist organizations, but, as more information developed, resistance to the plan spread through a substantial cross section of Nevada's population, especially in the Humboldt and mining regions, where most of the missile sites were scheduled to be located. Much vigorous criticism emerged from Reno as well; there was less in Las Vegas, presumably because the main operational base was to be located at Coyote Springs, about fifty miles north of that city, and the authorization of the MX would undoubtedly have meant another economic bonus for Clark County.

While Nevada considered the relative advantages (jobs and dollars) and disadvantages (damage to the traditional human and natural environment), a national debate erupted on the wisdom of the MX system as a whole. The idea of vehicles more massive than anything yet known, dragging 95-ton missiles along thousands of miles of newly constructed roads from one shelter to another, shocked hundreds of scientists, strategists, and moralists alike. And the cost—estimated conservatively at $30 billion and more commonly at $60 billion—startled even the richest of nations. Admiral Stansfield Turner, a leading military expert and former director of the Central Intelligence Agency, argued that the MX system was far too big and cumbersome to be effective; it would have the effect, he asserted, of making the threat of nuclear war greater rather than smaller.[17]

The *Bulletin of the Atomic Scientists,* one of the most influential scientific journals in the world, argued that not only would the MX be ineffective as a deterrent to attack, but it would also be obsolete before it could be completed (presumably before the end of the 1980s).[18] The Union of Concerned Scientists issued a bulletin in which it asserted that there were profound risks and unacceptable social consequences to be considered:

> A vast piece of real estate in Utah and Nevada will be taken from the Shoshone Indians, ranchers, miners, and close-knit Mormon communities. The 35,000 people who have chosen this independent life-style in the splendor of the Great Basin desert will find themselves a minority in their own communities and will find their communities transformed. This vast national resource will be destroyed needlessly.[19]

Nearer home, the Western Shoshone Indians, already involved in a legal controversy with the United States over title to 22 million acres of land, found a highly persuasive representative in Carrie Dann, who spoke with a powerful gentleness that won attention across the nation. Leaders of the Latter-day Saint church ultimately spoke out against the MX deployment proposal and asked that the land of their ancestors be allowed to continue in peace. A so-called Sagebrush Alliance of ranchers, miners, and other citizens—although poorly financed with meager contributions—created a network of opposition that grew into a majority position against the MX in Nevada by the end of 1980.

One of the organizations that did most to inform citizens about the potential impact was the Nevada Humanities Committee, which sponsored a series of lectures and discussions throughout the state and helped to create an awareness of the social and cultural consequences of turning the Great Basin into a vast missile arsenal. The committee helped to finance a film entitled "Battle-Born: MX in Nevada," which had national television distribution, with many Nevada residents speaking eloquently about this new challenge.

Because of recently enacted environmental protection laws, the Air Force was required to prepare and publicize an evaluation of the impact of its project on the region. Near the end of 1980, after having spent more than $17 million on the preparation of an environmental study, the Air Force released a 1,900-page Draft Environmental Impact Statement (DEIS) for public review. It was the release of this cumbersome document and its contents that brought the resistance to MX to a furious boil. The DEIS was highly technical in places and purported to survey the affected areas of Nevada and Utah, as well as potential sites under consideration in New Mexico and Texas. Nearly half of it related to the proposed Nevada deployment area, because under the Air Force's favorite plan, about two-thirds of the operation would have been based in Nevada.[20] It was offered to the public with the condition that any response must be made within 90 days. In addition to the main document, there were more than twenty-five technical supplements on various environmental problems and on plans to "mitigate" the adverse effects.

Many of us who worked on Nevada's official response to the DEIS gained a perspective of the state that had never been available before. The state government mounted an *ad hoc* response to the Air Force by forming thirty committees of state employees and other citizens, most of whom gave extra time and personal resources to the examination of the MX proposal. There was almost no state budget for the purpose, and the time limit—which was ultimately extended to 120 days instead of 90—rendered a thorough examination of all aspects of the problem almost impossible. But the nearly 400 Nevadans who contributed to the response to the DEIS were soon welded into the most effective analytical organization in the history of the state. Under the leadership of Stephen T. Bradhurst and his assistants, the committees of Nevadans divided the

Air Force document into specialized segments and analyzed each in detail. There were specialists in agriculture, anthropology, business, civil defense, energy, equal rights, fish and wildlife, geology, health and medicine, housing, journalism, labor, mining, planning, sanitation, soil, taxation, transportation, and utilities, among others. Miners, cattlemen, engineers, professors, Indian representatives, and citizens with a hundred other occupational specialties came together as a microcosm of the new Nevada that was emerging at the beginning of the fourth forty-year period in the state's history. Although the 1,200 pages that we produced are flawed in many ways because of the speed with which they were compiled, they represented a remarkable cooperative effort at defining the values and the resources of Nevada.[21]

In general, the DEIS had reiterated the promises of the Air Force spokesmen about keeping the environmental and social damage to a minimum, but the Nevada committees became convinced that the DEIS had not adequately considered the impact upon livestock, mining, and recreation business, on the wildlife, on water supplies, on historical and archeological resources, on state and local governments, on health services and schools, and so on. There was an overwhelming consensus that the "quality of life" would be irreparably damaged by the installation of the MX racetrack system.

Here, not among the cattlemen of the north or the politicians of Carson City, was the genuine sagebrush rebellion, a grass-roots reaction to a military mentality gone insane. Most of Nevada's politicians tended to follow, rather than to lead, public opinion in their reactions to the MX scheme. Governor Robert List, at first apparently neutral and cautious, eventually took the posture of an outspoken opponent after the public protest became widespread. Congressman Jim Santini became one of the early critics of MX and a useful conduit through whom many questions and objections got to Washington. Senator Howard Cannon, long an advocate of governmental projects that would bring dollars to Nevada and also a reserve general in the Air Force, gingerly supported the racetrack idea and ultimately alienated much of his constituency on that account. At one point in the public debate, he compared the potential impact of MX on Nevada with that of Hoover Dam in the 1930s. "Nevada has absorbed a huge construction project similar to MX in the past," he said. "We absorbed it and benefited from it, incorporating it into the history of our state's progress and prosperity."[22] This time, the invoking of those magic words "progress and prosperity" rang false. In the 1980 general election, eight counties held advisory referenda ballots on the question of whether the public approved MX, and the overwhelming majority in all counties cast negative ballots against the Air Force proposal.

In the autumn of 1981, after approximately two years of intensifying debate, President Reagan announced that the racetrack idea of deploying the missiles would be abandoned, primarily for the reason that even a system of widely distributed shelters could not be made safe from first-strike destruction under an enemy attack. While he announced that MX planning would go forward because such a missile was needed in the nation's arsenal, the method of deployment would have to be determined later. Senator Paul Laxalt, one of the president's closest friends and advisors, was widely believed to have exercised important influence against the plan to scatter the missiles across the two Great Basin states, but he insisted that the president had made his decision on strategic—not personal or political—grounds.

One argument that recurred often among the opponents of MX was that Nevada had already surrendered more of its land for defense uses than most other states and had therefore lost the possibility of future development for domestic purposes. By this time, the activities of one of the largest federal land users—the Atomic Energy Commission at the Nevada Test Site (NTS)—had become highly controversial.

The Nevada Test Site

Less than five years after the opening of the "atomic age," which was marked by the experimental explosions in New Mexico and the bombings of Hiroshima and Nagasaki in 1945, southern Nevada became the most active center in the world for the testing of atomic devices. Nevadans hardly noticed, in 1951, that they were suddenly playing host to the most ominous and awesome scientific experiments in the history of humankind.

Because the U.S. government was not content with the testing of atomic bombs in the Pacific Ocean, which it had done in the late 1940s, it brought them home to the least-populous, least-developed section of the continental United States for a series of atmospheric explosions. A section of the Las Vegas Bombing and Gunnery Range, consisting of 1,350 square miles north of Las Vegas, was selected rather quickly because it was believed to be safely distant from inhabited areas and secure from observation by potential enemies. Three large valleys— Yucca, Frenchman, and Jackass Flats—were sealed off from the rest of the country.

The first explosion occurred on January 27, 1951, and in the next quarter-century there were nearly 500 additional tests of various kinds, most of them atomic explosions for weapons-testing or for peaceful uses. In the first four years, scores of weapons were tested above ground, either exploded on towers or dropped from planes. Those who conducted the tests repeatedly told the public that they were safe, and there was at least superficial assurance that all precautions were being taken. Thousands of residents of southern Nevada and southern Utah wore monitoring badges to record the amount of radiation exposure, and there was no serious objection to the testing. The operations at NTS provided thousands of jobs in a short period of time for southern Nevada, which by now had come to take such windfalls from Washington for granted.

After several years of testing and badge reading, pressures from outside the state and nation brought a suspension of atmospheric testing; there was an ambiguous "backreading" of evidence that suggested that things might not be right with the downwind effects of the fallout. In 1963, the United States and the USSR signed a treaty mutually agreeing to forswear the right to test atomic weapons above ground. By that time, there had been hundreds of tests in Nevada and elsewhere. The long-range consequences of the explosions, some of which had carried radioactive clouds over populated areas, may not have been as fully understood as the Atomic Energy Commission thought them to be in the 1950s.

In the early 1980s, a thousand residents of southern Utah participated in a lawsuit against the U.S. government, charging that their dead relatives had been unwitting guinea pigs of a government experiment without adequate warnings of the dangers. Hundreds of people, it was charged, had died of cancer as a direct result of exposure to fallout from the tests.[23] The lawsuit followed a period of extended publicity and congressional investigations in which it was asserted that the federal government had deliberately suppressed information about the dangers of the tests. In May of 1984, Judge Bruce Jenkins ruled in Salt Lake City that ten people from southern Utah had indeed suffered from cancer caused by the fallout, that the government had not done an adequate job of protecting them, and that families of the victims—most of whom had died of cancer—were entitled to damages. The case, of course, went to the higher courts on appeal, and other similar cases were pending. Hundreds of people from eastern Nevada had made claims, as an unusual number of cancer-related deaths have occurred there in recent years.

It will require a versatile team of historians and scientists, after the lawyers and judges have done their best, to reach a definitive conclusion on the matter. The U.S. government has regularly affirmed that the greatest possible precautions were taken to ensure the safety of all concerned, but skepticism about such assurances was widespread, and it was a factor in the opposition to the MX propaganda that the Air Force distributed in 1981 and 1982.

One subordinate effect, or perhaps a primary benefit, of the Nevada Test Site operation has been to raise the level of awareness of those who consider the desert as a resource of more than pecuniary interest. A few individuals have come to think of spaces and species in terms of a broader biological ethic than the early pioneers had available to them when they were "conquering the wilderness." In 1976, Thomas O'Farrell and LaVerne Emery produced an ecological inventory of the life forms that exist in that delicate zone where the Great Basin and the Mohave deserts blend, with their high inland ranges and their low arid valleys, containing more than 700 kinds of plants and 1,000 invertebrates.[24] They augment what any dedicated prospector or member of the Sierra Club could affirm with only the slightest of prompting— that life is magnificently abundant even in this least profitable of deserts.

It is difficult to know what a layperson is to make of the plethora of information contained in technical reports of this kind, but the O'Farrell-Emery study seems to be a good one, well worth recommending for future reference. The experts who rely upon it for authorizations about future testing will be comforted by the assurance that "none of the species of flora and fauna is presently listed in the *Federal Register* as being either threatened or endangered." It is to be hoped that in the near future some comparable reassurance can be offered for *Homo sapiens*.

In 1957, when the last important lead-zinc-silver mines of eastern Nevada ceased production and left the miners of Pioche without work, some went southward to NTS to seek employment from the contractors who were digging the tunnels and caverns for the underground blasts. Many got good-paying jobs, because their skills were rare and well suited to the requirements of the Test Site contractors. In many cases the wages were far better than they had ever received in the mines and mills. But there was often a restlessness among the older men, who were unaccustomed to drilling, blasting, and slushing out the rock without looking for a pay-streak or commenting on the value of the ore. The vast amounts of money available for nuclear explosions puzzled the miners who had practiced their craft during the Depression years, and the vicissitudes of federal funding were far less understandable even than those of the erratic mining business.

One such miner was my father, who spent his life in Pioche and who, when the mines were down, went prospecting. He expressed his frustration in a letter when he was reacting to the typical conflicting rumors—of imminent layoffs and of vast new expansion programs. He was also writing a requiem for the frontier mining era and commenting on the emergence of a new kind of wilderness.

Mercury, Feb. 8, 1962

Dear Jim,

Your letter of the 4th was received yesterday and sure glad to get it.

Still unsettled here as to working. I think they are down to their last few millions.

I have some clippings cut out for you from the Vegas paper.

The noble Nevada Senators report on how we will double our expenditures beginning July 1st at the Nevada Test Site. It also mentions Cannon on space committee & the Rover Project will cost almost double the entire cost of Boulder Dam.

The low Nevada hills here rumble with shots from tunnels being bored. Also once in a while a bomb is set off underground. The A.E.C. and Defense cars are going here & there. And hundreds are parked around here & most of them burning gas while someone sits and talks with their heaters on and maybe a radio.

Security guards check you in & out everywhere. Kruchev could probably get farther than a good citizen.

Somewhere in this old desert some old prospector probably lies at rest in his grave. It is sure nice that he cannot wake up & see this mess. He probably came across the plains or around the Horn about 100 years ago.

He led his jackass from spring to spring & one mountain range to another and in no hurry he looked forward to the Bonanza that he was going to find.

His pickings were slim and at times he was mighty hungry, thirsty and cold. But he was happy. He made the old mountain his home & worked for others when his grub was low.

There is more money in one of these cigarette machines here than he ever saw in one whole year. His idea was to find and produce some new wealth for the country. He would be months from here to Beatty, Goldfield, Delamar, or Pioche. He would also have a good chance of finding a good vein of ore about 90 years ago.

He drilled by hand—blasted and mucked by hand. The jackass brayed & the desert was quiet and peaceful. Today the hills just rumble and roar, and the jets streak overhead & road blocks are set up to fire a bomb in some deep hole or tunnel.

Crews are driven hard to make footage & more tunnel. They must spend hundreds of millions to blow up more mountains. The job is urgent & must go on, part of it to cost twice as much as Boulder Dam. Why? To prepare ourselves for bankruptcy.

Thank God the old prospector can't wake up. Let him sleep. He did a good job. He covered every foot of the U.S.A. He made what wealth we have. The Comstock produced $800,000,000 & it was real money. They never had the great pieces of equipment we have today nor the vast sums of gvnt. money.

They saved the Union with the Gold and Silver.

These great brains today will prepare us for Communism when we go broke.

If a small amount of this money were used for real mining just 60 miles north at Goldfield or Tonopah or northeast at Pioche or Bristol about 90 miles or Groom 20 miles east, the possibilities are wonderful for a producer of great wealth to develop.

But mining is as dead as the old burro and the prospector.

It is sad to see the great ("Senators") brains of the State fall into a rut where several hundred million dollars will be burned up in Nevada and we can't get $4\frac{1}{2}$ million a year for lead-zinc subsidy.

If only Key Pittman and McCarran could attend our session of Congress now things would change. Gold and silver could revive and the mines & the whole West would prosper.

Today the tourist & our government expenditures are the total economy of the State.

Thank God the old prospector can rest forever.

This is probably pretty boring to you but it is hard to believe a great nation like ours can go to pot so easy. Who is going to produce anything, and what are they going to produce?

I work like hell here & produce absolutely nothing.

The waste and deliberate destruction is terrific & no one will ever change it now.

There wasn't a damn thing to write about so I give you my thoughts on NTS.

As ever,

Dad

CHAPTER 5

THE UTOPIA FOR GAMBLERS

WHEN MARK TWAIN was writing *Roughing It* about a century ago and reminiscing about his days in Nevada, he inserted a few lines that would need only the slightest modification to become applicable to the state in the contemporary era. He commented:

> In Nevada, for a time, the lawyer, the editor, the banker, the chief desperado, the chief gambler, and the saloon-keeper, occupied the same level in society, and it was the highest. The cheapest and easiest way to become an influential man and be looked up to by the community at large was to stand behind a bar, wear a cluster-diamond pin, and sell whisky. I am not sure but that the saloon-keeper held a shade higher rank than any other member of society. His opinion had weight. It was his privilege to say how the elections should go. No great movement could succeed without the countenance and direction of the saloon-keepers.[1]

Twain seems to have thought that he was commenting upon a passing phenomenon, but if he had used the example of the gambling house operator (and often he was the same as the saloon keeper) for his primary place of honor, his words would be as valid for the 1970s as they were for the 1860s.

Walter Van Tilburg Clark, in the most sensitive of his nonfictional examinations of the Nevada phenomenon, also reflected on the social values of the Comstock era.[2] His statements likewise suggest that the era of the Big Bonanza almost anticipated the era of the big casinos. Speaking of the people who lived in Virginia City in the early days, he wrote:

> It is unlikely that any other human community was ever more heedless of its surroundings, or more completely focused upon getting wealth, being amused when it wasn't getting wealth, and being in a hurry about both its work and its amusement.[3]

It is a generalization that might as appropriately have been made about the casino towns and their devotees a hundred years after the peak of the Comstock boom.

Gambling, like the state itself, is a creature of questionable birth and ancestry. It has had, since the beginning of Nevada history, the status of a bastard child, since it was pronounced an illegitimate activity in the earliest mining district regulations in the 1850s. It was illegal in Nevada in territorial days and in the first few years of statehood. It was legalized in 1869 and disowned again in 1910 at the time of the Progressive reform movements. It never quite disappeared in the railroad and mining towns, however; at best it went into the back rooms of the saloons. So there was a flourishing little stepchild business when the Depression induced the 1931 legislature to legitimize it, and ultimately the state began to nurture it like a prodigal son, to wrap the shawl of state sovereignty around it, and to assure the world that it was looking out for the morals and good conduct of its thriving adolescent. And the parent became increasingly dependent upon its progeny as the latter became larger, richer, and more famous and brought home a small share of its wealth to the family coffers. But the state could not avoid the suspicion, early in the 1980s, that it had become the slave and hostage of this multi-billion-dollar offspring of dubious reputation.

Nevada began to license and tax its casinos in a systematic way only in 1945, claiming 1 percent of the gross revenues. Over the years, as action increased and the pot got larger, the tax increased by stages to as much as 5¾ percent of the gross revenue for the larger casinos, and the dollar figures grew to astonishing proportions, like those in some inflated Monopoly game. And indeed the state did have a kind of monopoly on large-scale, statewide, legalized casino gambling for a third of a century.

In 1945, total gambling revenues were slightly more than $21 million; ten years later, they exceeded $110 million. By 1965, the figure was well above $300 million; by 1975, it had reached the billion dollar level.

In fiscal 1979–1980, the Gaming Control Board reported total winnings at $2.3 billion, and by this time virtually all of the state's politicians and planners had come to assume that a 10 to 20 percent annual rate of growth was part of the law of nature. The state government received, in tax revenue on the gross winnings, $118.4 millions in the 1979–1980 fiscal year, five hundred times as much as it had taken in 1945–1946. It had long since got into the habit of betting on the "come line" in a crap game that seemed to be a sure thing.

But at the end of the 1970s, two or three developments occurred almost simultaneously that undermined the self-confidence of the gambling operators and the Nevada government, which by this time had fallen into a parasitic relationship with the "industry." Other states and cities, attracted in part by Nevada's success in siphoning tax revenues from the gambling business, began to get into the act. The most aggressive rival was New Jersey, which licensed casinos on the Nevada model in Atlantic City, and thus provided an eastern alternative to Las Vegas and Reno. In addition, there was a larger cloud over the integrity of the gambling business in Nevada and the state's mechanism for policing it than there had ever been previously. Although it was widely acknowledged that most Nevada gamblers were honest and operated by the rules laid down by the gambling control authorities, the integrity of the state's control system itself was no longer taken for granted. And if the state could not certify that both the gambling business and its own agencies for supervising it were essentially honest, it could not expect the patronage of the millions of clients whom it had been attracting in recent years.

Assuring the world of the honesty of its "peculiar institution" is old business in Nevada. As early as 1940, less than ten years after gambling had been allowed to come out of the closet, the rationale for its existence had been worked out, and it has not varied much since. In the railroad towns and mining camps, it was seen as a legitimate social outlet for men who had worked hard all week and who deserved some old-fashioned frontier relaxation on Saturday night.

When the federal government distributed money to fight the Depression in the 1930s, it commissioned writers to produce history, social commentary, and travel information on the states, and the compilers of the Nevada book tried their hand at explaining the Nevada attitude on gambling. The rationale for gambling here is anonymous, but it may have been written by someone like Jeanne Elizabeth Wier, the venerable director of the Nevada Historical Society and the sponsor of the book:

> The Nevada attitude on gambling is further evidence of their lack of hypocrisy. . . . Like every other State in the Union, Nevada has always had its games of chance, and was no more successful than any other place in suppressing them. Faced with the great economic collapse and hunting for new sources of revenue that would not burden the population, it decided in 1931 to cut out the cost of ineffective attempts at suppression and at the same time increase State and local incomes by licensing the gambling devices. The law regulating open gambling had teeth, however, and the State keeps no gambling laws on its statute books that it does not enforce.[4]

This was almost certainly written by a Nevadan; it anticipated the kind of apology that was to become semiofficial as the business— euphemistically called an "industry" in Nevada—grew. Although there was virtually no supervision or control of the gambling enterprises in 1940 or for many years thereafter, it became common practice to assure both insiders and outsiders that everything was "on the up and up." Let us take note of one additional assurance that appeared in the official WPA guide of 1940:

> Further, the State is completely free of racketeers, in spite of the large sums handled by some of the clubs, and no Nevada prosecuting attorney has had a chance to make a name for himself by exposing corrupt relations between politicians and the gambling club owners.[5]

Our anonymous commentator is protesting too much. Like a cancer victim who suspects but cannot quite admit the possibility of a malignancy, Nevada continued to assure itself for decades that all was well, even when the growth of a strange parasitic tissue was evident.

The Evolution of Gambling Control

Although the Nevada Tax Commission began to license the gambling houses in the middle 1940s under the direct supervision of the governor, there was no agency to inquire into the suitability of applicants or to impose a standard of conduct upon them. During the administration of Governor Vail Pittman (1945–1950), gambling regulation was casual at best, and there was almost no attention given to the fact that many of the men who were building and operating the elaborate casinos in Las Vegas had criminal records elsewhere across the country. In 1947, the murder of Benjamin "Bugsy" Siegel, a prominent Las Vegas casino operator with gangland connections, caused a journalistic sensation, but this did not get translated into policy changes in Nevada.[6]

The state's political establishment was jarred from its lethargy by the nationwide investigations conducted by the U.S. Senate in 1950–1951 under the leadership of Senator Estes Kefauver of Tennessee. The Kefauver Committee looked into criminal activities in a dozen cities including Las Vegas, and it produced a "who's who" of Nevada gamblers and their connections with illicit activities elsewhere. Bugsy Siegel's gangster connections were already well known, and the past dealings with other licensees who were less notorious were not exactly secrets. But Kefauver's inventory of Las Vegas and Reno casino operators who had been associated with "rackets," "gangsters," and illegal gambling "syndicates" in other states strongly suggested that the associations with the criminal world were not all in the past. On the contrary, the obvious inference was that they were at that moment extensive and dangerous:

> Gambling profits are the principal support of big-time racketeering and gangsterism. These profits provide the financial resources whereby ordinary criminals are converted into big-time racketeers, political bosses, pseudo businessmen, and alleged philanthropists. . . .
>
> The legalization of gambling would not terminate the widespread predatory activities of criminal gangs and syndicates. The history of legalized gambling in Nevada and in other parts of the country gives no assurance that mobsters and racketeers can be converted into responsible businessmen through the simple process of obtaining state and local license for their gambling enterprises.[7]

That some casino operators had records for illegal gambling activities in other states came as no surprise in Nevada, but the extent of these connections and the adverse publicity associated with them were deeply troubling to the state's image-makers at that time. Kefauver's committee not only concluded that the "industry" was nourishing the crime syndicates but that there were questionable relationships between the gamblers and the state officers who had some responsibility for supervising their operations. Lieutenant Governor Clifford Jones and William Moore, the latter a member of the Nevada Tax Commission, which supervised the gambling business, were themselves licensees and part owners in Las Vegas casinos.[8]

The Kefauver report eventually did lead to some minor adjustments in gambling control policy to eliminate the most obvious conflicts of interest, but in a larger sense it had the opposite effect in Nevada from the one its authors wanted; it wedded the state even more closely to the special "industry" and made its leaders more protective of it. Senator Pat

McCarran, who was no admirer of legalized gambling but an instinctive defender of the state's financial well-being, used his considerable influence in the Senate Judiciary Committee and elsewhere in Washington to block Kefauver's efforts to impose a crippling federal tax upon the gamblers. He wrote: "It isn't a very laudable position for one to have to defend gambling. One doesn't feel very lofty when his feet are resting on the argument that gambling must prevail in the State that he represents. . . ." But McCarran's political instincts told him that it was necessary "to call upon every source of assistance, good, bad and indifferent" however much he might regret the obligation.[9] And his successors in high political office followed his example, usually without expressing any such misgivings.

For a quarter of a century after the Kefauver investigation, Nevada was fortunate to have men of high integrity in the governor's office, for it was there that the responsibility for honest gambling control ultimately resided. The governor appointed the members of the gambling control agencies and set the guidelines for policy. The legislature normally meets only for three or four months every other year, so the role of this branch in gambling control was small. While there were many controversies and occasional outbursts of bad publicity, the occupants of the chief executive's office avoided any serious accusations of impropriety for themselves and their appointees. Much of the administrative work was transferred to a Gaming Control Board in 1955, under a fiscal and investigatory system designed largely by Robbins Cahill, chairman of the Nevada Tax Commission. Nevada appeared to be getting its peculiar "industry" under tighter supervision and building defenses against the infiltration of more criminal elements.

The Thunderbird Case

A crucial test of the state government's ability to exercise its police powers over the gambling business came in the middle 1950s in the celebrated Thunderbird Hotel case, when a group of Las Vegas gambling licensees challenged the regulatory authority of the Tax Commission and, in effect, tried to bend all three constitutional branches of the state government to their will. For a short time, the Thunderbird owners held the leadership of the Democratic party in their grip and tried to dictate their terms to the Supreme Court.

The test came during the administration of Governor Charles Russell (1951–1958), a quiet, methodical administrator who relied heavily upon

Cahill. When Russell and Cahill learned that some notorious underworld figures, unacceptable under the state's post-Kefauver regulations, had secret financial ties with the Thunderbird owners, they moved to revoke the gambling license of the operators.

The main owner of the hotel-casino was Marion Hicks, a long-time Nevada businessman, and a lesser owner was Lieutenant Governor Jones, who had already received close scrutiny from the Kefauver Committee. Jones was a Democrat and a political ally of former governor Vail Pittman, who was twice the Democratic opponent of Republican Russell for the governorship. The second of their electoral contests occurred in 1954 and coincided with the beginning of the Thunderbird case. The *Las Vegas Sun,* the flamboyant, crusading newspaper owned by Hank Greenspun, published a series of startling articles asserting that there was tape-recorded evidence showing that Jones hoped—after the anticipated election of Pittman—to remove Cahill from office and weaken the Tax Commission's regulatory power.[10]

In 1955, after Russell had defeated Pittman for the second time, the Tax Commission, with the tape-recorded evidence in hand, voted to revoke the license of the Thunderbird, only to be blocked when Hicks and Jones obtained a district court order from a rural judge, restraining the commission from exercising its police powers. It appeared initially only to be a partisan political matter—a Republican governor and his Tax Commission taking revenge against a Democratic lieutenant governor and his allies. But as the case made its way to the Supreme Court and into the 1957 legislative session, it became evident that a much more fundamental issue was at stake. Did the Tax Commission have the power to suspend summarily the license of a casino suspected of illicit activity or of having criminal associations, or was it necessary to prove all its suspicions in a court trial before a gambling license could be revoked?

In the 1957 session of the legislature, while the case of *Tax Commission* v. *Hicks* was pending before the Nevada Supreme Court, friends of Jones and Hicks introduced a bill in the Nevada Senate that proposed to strip virtually all power from the Tax Commission and its enforcement agency, the Gaming Control Board, and to put primary responsibility for gambling license review and revocation in the courts. In other words, the Tax Commission would have retained the ability to gather evidence and to hear testimony, but not finally to revoke the license of an operating gambler before having a trial *de novo* in a court of law—often a long, slow process. Such a law would have given an undesirable gambler—even a cheating or fraudulent operator—months of immunity from punitive action while the case was proceeding through the commission and the courts.

The bill was drafted with a preamble that presumed to interpret the earlier statutes in favor of the gamblers; it was clearly intended to give instruction to the Supreme Court about the intentions of previous sessions of the legislature. Labeled S.B. 92, this measure became the most controversial piece of legislation ever introduced in the century-long history of gambling in Nevada. Its rodeo-like ride through the capitol halls—where every Democrat in both houses voted for it—to the governor's desk for the anticipated veto and back to the Senate, made legislative history and turned out to be a decisive test of Nevada's will to exercise a measure of control over its casino operators.

S.B. 92, introduced in the Senate, had emerged from committee and had won floor approval with only perfunctory consideration in the closing days of the session. It had twelve supporters and five opponents—more than the two-thirds majority necessary to override the expected veto from Governor Russell. It reached the Assembly, the lower house of the legislature, only a week before the constitutional deadline for the closing of the session. Its supporters faced the challenge of passing the bill at least five days before the end of the session so that when the governor did veto it, there would be sufficient time to return it to the legislature and override the veto.

Hicks, Jones, and their allies had done their work well. They persuaded the Assembly Judiciary Committee, to which S.B. 92 had been assigned, to yield it to the full Assembly without consideration, and they mobilized all the Democrats in the Assembly (many of whom did not like it) to support it as a partisan matter. The Assembly had thirty-two Democrats and fifteen Republicans—barely the two-thirds majority necessary to defeat the veto. On a straight party-line vote, the Democrats rushed the bill to final passage in an after-midnight emergency session, approved it 32–13, and rushed it to the governor.

Robert Vaughan, a freshman assemblyman from Elko, became the leader of the minority effort to delay the bill and to provide more opportunity for public discussion. His efforts, publicized in the newspapers of the state, became a summons to a broad contingent of citizens to support the state's announced policy of tight administrative control for gambling houses. Speaking to his fellow legislators at 2:00 A.M. on a cold March morning as he was trying to delay passage of the bill, Vaughan issued a warning that won attention well beyond the walls of the chamber:

I fear that if this act becomes law there are large sums of gambling money that may go into the election campaigns of judges, even to the judges on the district level. You can see the magnitude of the problems when you realize what has happened today. One man or a few men in the State took control of the entire Legislature and is assuring the passage of this law in the interest of a few gamblers with special problems and not in the interest of the gambling industry as a whole. You can see what effect this might have on the judiciary where you have one judge at a salary of $15,000 per year with the discretion of closing or leaving open a gambling establishment. . . .

Vaughan worried not only about the corruption that might occur in the judicial branch—which had previously enjoyed a reputation for high integrity—but also about the possibility that the destruction of administrative control would lead to the eventual death of the"industry" and the loss of millions of dollars of state revenue.[11] Thus he, like most of his fellow political figures after his time, based his appeal in part on the need to "protect" the gambling business from its own bad apples.

Governor Russell vetoed the bill as expected, but since it had passed both houses with enough votes to override, it appeared that S.B. 92 would become law, the administrative machinery for supervising gambling would be severely weakened, and the courts would be clogged with regulatory responsibilities. At the crucial hour, however, Senator Ralph Lattin of Fallon, who originally voted for the bill, switched his position to support the governor, thus sustaining the veto. It was a singular act of courage without parallel in the history of the legislature, and while a few of his colleagues in the Senate scorned him for a time, he was ultimately honored widely in the state for his act.

That a single vote had prevented the dismantling of Nevada's gambling control apparatus came as a shock to much of the citizenry. The Nevada legislature has always been small—between fifty and seventy-five members—and a relatively small group has occasionally been able to exercise much influence within and upon it. But there has never been a full explanation for the fact that the Thunderbird Hotel contingent was able to organize and control, at least for a short time, all the Democrats in the legislature. The casino owners had managed to convince the party leadership, together with their allies in organized labor, that gambling licensees were suffering a grievous wrong because they were vulnerable to a capricious administrative agency. They nearly altered the law decisively, even though most other gambling operators in Las Vegas and Reno registered their opposition to S.B. 92.

As one of the newspaper reporters who covered the events of the 1957 session, I shared the impression that a narrow but crucial victory had been won for the cause of "clean" gambling. There was a widespread sense that a courageous governor and a minority of dedicated legislators had saved Nevada's special "industry," and thus had benefited the state.

Soon after the legislature adjourned in the spring of 1957, the Supreme Court handed down its decision in the case of *Tax Commission* v. *Hicks* and reaffirmed the principle that gambling was a tolerated nuisance in Nevada, subject to the police powers of an administrative agency and not entitled to trial proceedings *de novo*. It found, however, that in trying to revoke the Thunderbird's license two years earlier, the commission had not followed its own guidelines, so the court allowed the continued operation of the hotel-casino. The Thunderbird had in the meantime purged itself of the affiliation with the underworld figures. The ruling was, in a sense, a victory for both sides, but it left the state's policing power intact. The decision contained a statement by its author, Justice Charles Merrill, that echoed the findings of Kefauver and should have served as a warning to the people of the state:

> We note that while gambling, duly licensed, is a lawful enterprise in Nevada, it is unlawful elsewhere in this country; that unlawfully followed elsewhere it tends there to create as well as to attract a criminal element; that it is a pursuit which, unlawfully followed, is conducive of corruption; that the criminal and corruptive elements engaged in gambling tend to organize and thus obtain widespread power over corruptive criminal enterprises throughout this country; that the existence of organized crime has long been recognized and has become a serious concern of the federal government as well as the governments of the several states.
>
> Throughout this country, then, gambling has necessarily surrounded itself with an aura of crime and corruption. Those in management of this pursuit who have succeeded, have done so not only through a disregard of law, but, in a competitive world, through a superior talent for such disregard and for the corruption of those in public authority.
>
> For gambling to take its place as a lawful enterprise in Nevada it is not enough that this state has named it lawful. We have but offered it the opportunity for lawful existence. The offer is a risky one, not only for the people of this state, but for the entire nation. Organized crime must not be given refuge here through the legitimatizing of one of its principal sources of income. Nevada gambling, if it is to succeed as a lawful enterprise, must be free from the criminal and corruptive taint acquired by gambling beyond our borders. If this is to be accomplished not only must the operation of gambling be carefully controlled, but the character and background of those who would engage in gambling in this state must be carefully scrutinized.[12]

Never has a Nevadan spoken more responsibly about the strange experiment that the state had undertaken in desperation during the Depression years. Unfortunately, Justice Merrill's words were dicta, widely approved but not easily translated into public policy.

"Hanging Tough"

For several years after the "close call" of 1957, the impression grew that Nevada had begun to take control of its gambling business. Governor Russell's successor, Grant Sawyer (1959–1966), guided an administrative reorganization plan through the legislature, removing responsibility for gambling control from the Tax Commission and creating a separate Gaming Commission, Gaming Control Board, and later a Policy Board, all with specialized functions. New statutes specifically empowered state agents to inspect and examine the premises, equipment, supplies, books, and records of the gambling houses and to undertake thorough investigations of all applicants for licenses. Governor Sawyer set the tone of his eight-year term with a directive to his commissioners and board members soon after he took office:

> You will be subject to almost unbelievable pressures. I know you cannot be bought with money. I am sure you will not let social or political considerations affect your actions.
>
> My feeling, to state it briefly, is this. Get tough and stay tough. A gambling license is a privilege—it is not a right. If you err, err on the side of rigidity rather than laxity. Hang tough and you will be doing a great service to me, to the industry, and to the state.[13]

The "hang tough" policy received much publicity and kept the Sawyer administration relatively free from controversy until near the end of his tenure, but the suspicions of well-informed outsiders did not diminish. In 1963, Wallace Turner, an investigative reporter for the *New York Times,* published a series of articles on the connections between Nevada's legal casinos and the crime syndicates; his findings appeared in a book about two years later.[14] The money generated by the Nevada gambling houses, Turner concluded, was "a new force in American life, a force for evil."[15]

Turner contended that several Nevada casinos were "skimming" some of their huge profits for out-of-state criminal interests before reporting their revenues to Nevada or federal authorities. These untaxed profits were "a cancerous growth on the American moral fiber." He chronicled the connections between the casinos and the Teamsters' pension fund, with scandals that touched the American Stock Exchange, the secretary of the United States Senate, Chicago mobs, and questionable gambling operations abroad. His book was the most comprehensive indictment of the gambling business since the Kefauver investigation; it ended with an impassioned plea that gambling be contained within Nevada and not be allowed to pollute the fiber of the nation any further than it was already doing. But it had little impact either within or outside the state.

As gambling and the state's efforts to create a credible policing mechanism escalated, some familiar jurisdictional confrontations occurred. Governor Sawyer, dedicated to the principle of tight state control, ran afoul of the agents of J. Edgar Hoover's Federal Bureau of Investigation, who were in Las Vegas pursuing some of the minions of organized crime. Hoover's G-men, occasionally insensitive to the principles of civil liberties inscribed in the Bill of Rights, spied on and taped their subjects in a manner that conflicted both with common decency and with Nevada's anti-bugging laws. Governor Sawyer, who was genuinely "tough" on crime and suspicious of racketeering, took offense at FBI procedures that employed some of the same tactics that the underworld had adopted as stock-in-trade, and he protested to Washington.[16] Sawyer and Hoover exchanged charges and insults that were at least as vitriolic as any they directed against the elusive criminals. In the surrealistic aura that surrounded legalized gambling, the standard rules of American politics and jurisprudence seemed to be in suspension.

Who had primary responsibility for controlling crime and mob-related gambling, and what procedures were most appropriate? This was a fundamental question, and it went beyond the tentative explorations of the Kefauver Committee and the arguments of Wallace Turner. In 1966, Sawyer was in a political struggle for reelection, and J. Edgar Hoover was trying desperately to hold onto his police-state style of FBI administration, which was incompatible with the basic principles of American constitutional law. At one point Governor Sawyer proposed the prosecution of FBI agents who had violated Nevada wire-tapping laws; the FBI refused to share with the state evidence that suggested criminal infiltration of the gambling industry. A series of articles in the *New York Times* and the *Washington Post,* among other widely distributed periodicals, kept the nation informed about this peculiar wrinkle in federal-state relations. The 1966 election brought a hiatus but not a solution to this impass, because Governor Sawyer lost his bid for reelection to Lieutenant Governor Paul Laxalt, who favored Hoover's position.

In the meantime, Las Vegas continued to flourish as though it were oblivious to the blizzard of controversy that had descended upon its favored "industry." Jimmy Hoffa of the Teamsters' Union, which had invested huge amounts of retirement money in the casinos, made an ostentatious appearance at the opening of a $25-million showplace— Caesar's Palace—as if to emphasize that none of the furor affected him.[17]

At the same time that the struggle between Hoover and Sawyer was underway, Nevada's fiscal planners took another look at gambling revenue and concluded that the "industry" could pay higher taxes to help finance the state's growing social needs. A movement initiated by two rural county legislators, Ray Knisley of Lovelock and Cyril Bastian of Caliente, in a 1966 special session of the legislature bore fruit the following year, when the assessment formula was changed to increase gambling taxes by approximately 20 percent. While the move was initially opposed by most Clark County legislators and most casino operators, they adjusted to it rapidly, and both the gamblers' net income and the state treasury improved. For a few years, the state supported its social programs and a long-neglected, rapidly growing educational system at a better level than ever before.

Paul Laxalt and Howard Hughes

The administration of Governor Laxalt (1967–1970) produced several new departures in gambling policy. The Nevada Gaming Commission closed two large casinos on charges of cheating during Laxalt's first year in office, reinforcing the belief that Nevada was indeed clearing its house of hoodlums. The Nevada Resort Association, consisting of eleven of the major Las Vegas casinos, paid for the publication of a twelve-part series of articles in the Las Vegas and Reno newspapers to explain their financial procedures and problems.[18] Never had any group of casino operators been so willing to discuss publicly their financial situation and their debt structures. In addition, the Laxalt years saw the entrance of Howard Hughes into the Nevada gambling arena and the introduction of corporate gambling licenses, which built the kind of connection between Las Vegas and Wall Street that Wallace Turner had warned against a few years earlier.

Hughes had been fond of Las Vegas during World War II and had visited the town in the 1950s when he was still an enterprising industrialist and promoter. By the time of his mysterious return in 1966, when his advance-men rented the ninth floor of the Desert Inn on the

Strip and carried him there secretly at night, he was one of the wealthiest and most eccentric men in the world. In his own view, most of his business enterprises had been failures, in spite of the fact that he had accumulated billions of dollars. Possessed by a deep sense of depression and a desperate need for privacy, he came to Las Vegas, of all places, to hide from the pressures of the world while he manipulated his financial empire. According to his leading biographers, his spirits were revitalized by his decision to buy control of the Desert Inn, after its owner had tried to evict him, and to apply his legendary financial skills to the Nevada landscape.[19]

Hughes spent four years closeted in his ninth-floor penthouse on the Strip. Almost no one, not even most of his closest associates, saw him as he indulged himself in a neurotic desire for privacy while he built a Nevada financial empire. He bought five more gambling houses in Las Vegas and one in Reno, creating one of the state's largest casino networks. He purchased a television station, an airport, and hundreds of mining claims. The size of his Nevada holdings was estimated at between $125 and $500 million.

At first most Nevadans who had anything to say about Hughes—officials and mavericks alike—sang his praises. Governor Laxalt repeatedly spoke of the benefits that Hughes and his investments brought to the state, and Hank Greenspun, the cynical editor of the *Las Vegas Sun,* for a long time accorded him much greater deference than he usually granted to gamblers and public figures. Hughes took an early, generous interest in some serious state problems. When the 1967 legislature was quarreling over the establishment of a medical school at the University of Nevada in Reno, he turned the tide in favor of the proposal by pledging between $200,000 and $300,000 per year for twenty years to support it. Later he made another contribution to help the university initiate a community college system.[20]

It was commonly believed that Hughes had undertaken a personal crusade to cleanse Nevada gambling of its undesirable elements. In some of the casinos that he purchased, there were believed to be part owners or operators with ties to the criminal underground, and Hughes replaced several of them. Soon after he had appeared on the scene, several large publicly owned corporations, including Metro-Goldwyn-Mayer, Hilton Hotels, Holiday Inns, the Del Webb Corporation, and others, began to invest in the Nevada gambling-tourist business, encouraged by a new Laxalt policy that made it possible for broadly owned conglomerates to obtain gambling licenses. William Harrah, whose large casinos at Reno and Lake Tahoe had long been regarded as models of honest operations, "went public," turning his private holdings into a corporation and offering shares on the New York Stock Exchange.

In the meantime, as the Hughes investments within the state grew, there was increasing evidence of financial trouble. He began to lose money, either because of fiscal mismanagement by himself or his associates or because his reticence made him vulnerable to misappropriation of his resources. By 1970, his last year in Nevada, a bitter power struggle occurred within his organization, culminating in a plot by some of his associates to spirit him out of Las Vegas to the Bahamas without the knowledge of other associates.[21] Governor Laxalt tried to intervene and mediate because he had become convinced that the trouble within the Hughes organization threatened to retard the state's rapid economic growth, which Hughes had apparently done much to accelerate. The affairs of his companies had become so intimately entangled with those of the gambling business that state authorities found it necessary to pursue him into his other hiding places after he left Nevada and to join the struggle over his estate after his death in 1976. At one point, in March of 1973, Governor Mike O'Callaghan and Chairman Philip Hannifan of the Gaming Control Board traveled to London to interview him in a darkened bedroom.[22]

The Hughes sojourn in Nevada was a mixed blessing. It obviously improved the state's economy and gave a much-desired film of respectability to the industry. Only somewhat later did it appear that the struggle within the Hughes organization, which involved some of his older advisors against the newer ones, some local financial institutions, and prominent members of the Latter-day Saint (Mormon) church, was almost as unsavory as the struggle among the "hoods" whom he had presumably replaced. "Ultimately," one recent study concluded, "the whole Hughes episode served as an example, not of the 'new' Las Vegas, but of the old con game extended to some new players."[23] When Hughes died in 1976, pitifully emaciated by malnutrition and overindulgence in drugs, this most bizarre chapter in the history of a bizarre business came to an end. There were a few sequels in the court as heirs and claimants fought over the assets and the various wills that emerged, and the state of Nevada felt obliged to intervene to protect its legacy from Hughes for the medical school. The gambling empire that he had built continued to function and to grow for the next few years at least as well as it had done during his lifetime.

The Nevada public, basking in the new prosperity, was disposed to tell itself that the benefits of the Hughes reign outweighed the problems and the embarrassment, and the assumption was that the new era of

corporate gambling assured respectability. When Robert Laxalt, one of
the state's most skillful and successful creative writers, prepared the
bicentennial history of the state for the American Association of State
and Local History, there seemed to be good justification for echoing the
conventional assurances about the reform of the industry. In discussing
the Las Vegas Strip, he acknowledged the basic facts about the previous
era:

> In one way or another, most of the hotels were owned by the underworld,
> but there was no getting at the truth of who really owned what. With their
> highly developed antennae for anticipating trouble, bosses of crime syn-
> dicates were already resorting to the device of placing reasonably "clean"
> puppets out in front.[24]

He routinely chronicled instances of gangland style murders within and
outside Nevada, but concluded that the imposition of tough restrictions
and supervision by a series of governors had solved the problem. Philip
Hannifan, still chairman of the Gaming Control Board, said the current
regulations were based upon a "model arrived at through painful trial
and error in the face of what once seemed insurmountable odds," and he
administered the usual sedative on this occasion by remarking that the
FBI, the IRS, the Securities and Exchange Commission, and the Interstate Commerce Commission all had roles in supervising the legal
games of chance or their owners. "With all that scrutiny, you have to
believe that the hoodlum presence in Nevada is either gone or so
minimal that it doesn't count for much."[25]

Most Nevadans were willing to accept this judgment, at least until the
late 1970s. Another quotation from Laxalt's book—the first publication
by a Nevadan, incidentally, to look so candidly at the problem—
provided yet another reassurance:

> What is rarely mentioned is the fact that underlying the success of
> gambling control has been the innate incorruptibility of the individuals
> who govern gambling in Nevada. Since the formation of the Gambling
> Control Board, there has not been a breath of scandal attached to gambling-
> law enforcement in Nevada.[26]

There were several instances in the early 1970s when the state's
gambling control agencies acted decisively against operators suspected
of skimming, bribery, or conspiracy to conceal criminal elements in
specific casinos. The conviction of several gamblers under Nevada law

gave credence to the analysis that Laxalt offered his readers in the bicentennial year. It was possible, in that happy year of reawakened patriotism, to believe that Nevada, in spite of its wayward past, had become respectable and had made its gambling business good, clean fun. Only about a year after the publication of this book, however, the "innate incorruptibility" of those responsible for gambling control came under a cloud. It was not the Gaming Control Board or the Gaming Commission, however, that suffered a tarnished image, but the governor himself.

The Rude Reawakening

Only a few days after the 1978 election, the governor-elect, Robert List, the man who would have primary responsibility for appointing the top personnel for gambling control for the next four years, admitted that while serving as attorney general in the recent past he had accepted free rooms and meals from a Las Vegas resort hotel while his office was engaged in court proceedings against the hotel's parent corporation and one of its associates who was said to have had ties with organized crime. It was revealed that the governor-elect not only had received "comps"—slang for "complimentary services"—for more than $2,000 from the gambling establishment against whose owners he was litigating, but also that he had received reimbursement from the state for the same expenses. List asserted that there was nothing unusual in his acceptance of the favors from an organization against which he was directing a lawsuit, since gambling establishments "write off" more than $100 million annually from their taxes as "comps." "Certainly if a public official were going to sell out, he would not do it for the price of a room and a meal," List said.[27] There was nothing illegal in his action under Nevada law, but this was a stunning rationalization for Nevadans who had come to think of their gambling control officers as people of the highest principles.

This and a number of other episodes cast a shadow over the sunny reassurances that Nevada's officials had been giving about the cleanliness of the "industry." When New Jersey prepared for the introduction of legalized gambling in Atlantic City in 1978 and 1979, questions arose once again about the possibility of "mob infiltration" of Nevada from that area. The Justice Department's Organized Crime Strike Force seemed to lead to the doorsteps of some Las Vegas resorts, and the FBI filed affidavits in Kansas City purporting to connect the crime rings there with Las Vegas.[28] Shortly thereafter, the Gannett newspapers of

Reno published a long series of articles on the troubled gambling control agencies of Nevada and concluded that Nevada's highly touted system of supervision was "mostly show," in need of improvements if it were to transform its largely "cosmetic" regulation into more forceful supervision.[29]

The articles had little apparent result. Nevadans were eager once again to return to the pattern of reassuring themselves and others that matters were not truly out of control. In January of 1980, Governor List assured the Reno Chamber of Commerce that Nevada had "really turned the corner" in removing organized crime from the "industry."[30] Although it was acknowledged that the FBI had uncovered criminal connections with five Las Vegas casinos, it appeared that a true remedy was at hand. In the spring of 1981, a few of the gambling-resort operators tried to organize a statewide observance in honor of the fiftieth anniversary of the 1931 relegalization of games of chance, and Governor List participated in the celebration. In an address he described Nevada's experience with gambling as "the great experiment that worked." "Over the past five decades," he said, "the once-backroom activities have stepped boldly to the forefront, becoming the legitimate economic staple of our beloved Silver State."[31]

The insensitivities of former attorney general (later governor) List and his testimonials on behalf of the gambling business had little effect on the flow of events as Nevada finished the first half-century of its peculiar experiment with the "industry." The mechanism of gambling control appears to have functioned about as effectively in his administration as it had done previously, but by this time the business was so much larger and the opportunities for abuse of the privileges so much greater that the stakes and the dangers were enormous. Like a cowboy who had gone into an evening poker game for recreation and found the pots getting bigger and bigger, Nevada was "in over its head" and did not quite know what to do about it. List's defeat in a bid for his second term as governor in 1982 probably had little to do with any question about the propriety of his actions vis-à-vis his responsibility in gambling control; it probably resulted from an ill-conceived "tax reform" program that was the inverse side of the Nevada coin.

For List had built upon the work of his predecessors in making the state treasury ever more dependent on the tourist trade and the gambling revenues. He had designed a budget built even more completely on the expectation of rising gambling and sales taxes, paid in large part by the tourists who had been lured to our valleys for "Nevada-style" fun. During the year in which he was elected governor, the Civil Aeronautics

Board deregulated the interstate airline business and thereby introduced an immediate windfall for Nevada's casinos, because several airline companies quickly added the gambling cities to their routes. Reno, whose business leaders had felt themselves to be economically hog-tied for years because of the regulation, soon found itself served by ten airlines instead of three and by sixty-five flights a day instead of thirty-eight.

The recession of 1981–1982 changed all that; at about the time of the celebration of the fiftieth anniversary of legalized gambling, revenues from the slot machines and tables began to fall sharply. For more than a year, Nevada felt the pinch of the national recession in a way that was unfamiliar to the younger two-thirds of the population. The state treasury, long accustomed to comfortable surpluses, was nearly empty, and in the middle of the fiscal year the governor's office called for spending reductions of 15 to 20 percent below the appropriated level. Unemployment, which had traditionally been low in the neon boomtowns, was higher than the national average for several months. It seemed time for a reassessment of the state's priorities, and that might have come to pass had the recession been a bit longer or memories not quite so short.

As Others See Us

In the middle of the 1970s, Jerome Skolnick, a California sociologist, did an intensive scholarly investigation of the Nevada casino business from within. He evaluated the psychological and social consequences of Nevada's commitment to a business that was commonly regarded as a vice. He titled his book, appropriately, *House of Cards*.[32] After exploring the question of whether gambling is a form of play or of pathology, he offered one of the most thorough descriptions of casino procedures in popular print and described the workings of the Nevada gambling control organizations. He concluded that organized crime had not been eradicated; it persisted successfully because it was able to remain out of sight most of the time. But he went further than most observers who had previously reached this conclusion. He compared the model of Nevada gambling—which he expected to be adopted by other states then considering legalization—with gambling in Britain.

At the time he made his observations in Britain, gambling was regarded as an evil that should not be driven underground, but, on the other hand, it was not social policy to encourage it; in Nevada, it is promoted and encouraged because it is a significant source of governmental revenue. The British officials deplored the vice and sought to restrict the demand for it; a person who wanted to gamble was required to declare an intention to do so in writing at least forty-eight hours in advance, so that impulsive betting would be discouraged. Live entertainment was not permitted in British gambling establishments, and they were not allowed to extend credit to their clients. In Nevada, all the surroundings, rules, and attractions are designed to get the bettors— large and small—to relax their inhibitions and their purse strings.[33]

The basic difference between the British and the Nevada approaches to gambling, Skolnick argued, arises from the fact that Nevada has become so totally dependent on the "industry." Unlike the British, who at the time he wrote were not seeking to gain any revenue from its operation, Nevada must adapt its public policy and its standards to meet the needs of the casinos. He commented: "The overriding political question is no longer whether gambling should be legal, but what sorts of legislative policy—what structure of legalization—will enhance the prosperity of the industry." Nevada will not, for example, outlaw gambling credit from the casino business, even though demonstrably it invites organized crime onto the scene and enables the hoodlums to hide their gains.[34] This line of argument suggested that even if the Nevada gambling control organization were managed by the most honest of people, it would not be possible to adopt procedures that would eradicate the criminal element because such procedures might be construed as damaging the "industry" itself. During the 1970s, nearly every large Las Vegas casino was touched by scandal, and several gambling club operators were convicted of crimes, but it apparently made no difference to the public.

Skolnick predicted that casino gambling would become more vulnerable to public indignation, criminal infiltration, and ultimately federal control if and when it spread to other states—as it was beginning to do when he wrote. The "industry" may, he wrote, contain the "seeds of its own destruction." And he added (this was written late in the second term of Governor O'Callaghan):

> I have encountered in Nevada some of the most able, honest, and aggressive public administrators one could imagine. The presence of such people also makes clear how easy it is to undermine the administrative controls merely by appointing inept, even if honest, officials to key positions.[35]

Whether or not casino gambling was an endangered species because of the uncertainties of the control mechanism and the continuing presence of organized crime, it had helped to create a new set of American values in the middle years of the twentieth century. Las Vegas had taken over Hollywood stars and images—the ingredients of the fantasy world that America loved in the 1930s and 1940s—and had employed them in the service of its industry. The sex symbols and comedians of the movies happily made the trip from Hollywood to the Strip for the big money and thus put their art and their prestige at the service of those who profited most from the betting fever that they helped to induce.

Probably the most celebrated example of the Las Vegas/Hollywood connection is the Frank Sinatra case. Affiliated with a gambling operation in Las Vegas and Lake Tahoe casinos in the 1950s, Sinatra had his gambling license revoked in 1963 during the "hang-tough" days of Governor Sawyer because he allegedly maintained contacts in his casino operations with an underworld figure who was on the state's "black list." He engaged in a bitter exchange of accusations with the state's gambling control officials. In 1981, when Sinatra sought a license once again during Governor List's term, it was obvious that the old troubles, if not completely forgotten, were at least easily brushed aside. During the new hearings, Sinatra called some of Hollywood's most adored personalities as character witnesses, and the national news media reported that he had the support of the most famous Hollywood personality of all, Ronald Reagan. Sinatra had no trouble getting a license on that occasion.[36]

The eclectic writer Tom Wolfe, who exploded onto the literary scene as one of the leading interpreters of the new "pop culture" in the 1960s, called Las Vegas the Versailles of post–World War II America:

> . . . long after Las Vegas influence as a gambling heaven is gone, Las Vegas' forms and symbols will be influencing American life. That fantastic skyline! Las Vegas' neon sculpture, its fantastic fifteen-story-high display signs, parabolas, boomerangs, rhomboids, trapezoids and all the landscape outside the oldest parts of the oldest cities. They are all over every suburb, every subdivision, every highway. . . .[37]

Las Vegas seemed to Wolfe to offer the ultimate experiences in electronic and sensual stimulation, in the possibilities for pandering to the fantasies of the middle-aged. It tempted people to press their senses to the limit, with pep pills, depressants, and liquor, between the shows and the betting. It was the epitome of modern America's desire to escape responsibility and to enjoy.[38]

The problem with Wolfe's freewheeling tribute/indictment of Las Vegas is not exaggeration, although there is some of that; the problem is that his portrait of Las Vegas was and is essentially valid. Born of Nevada's frontier heritage and nourished by its political "sovereignty," Las Vegas—and to a lesser extent Reno—has helped to create and transmit new cultures and values across the land—or perhaps they are very old cultures and values. They are those of the old wilderness, of savagery and self-indulgence, which civilizations for at least four thousand years have been trying to tame and to modify. We have licensed a good deal more than gambling in Nevada, and in the process of conquering one wilderness we have created another, far more threatening than the original.

CHAPTER 6

BEYOND THE GLITTER: A STATE WITHOUT
A CONSCIENCE

HAS THE MUCH-PUBLICIZED revenue from gambling and tourism en-
riched Nevada in any way except financially? What does the state have
to show for its half-century of legalized vice? Are the so-called normalcy
and the domestic conservatism of its neighborhoods and rural communities truly immune from the ethical standards, the commercial
techniques, and the psychedelic stimulation that Tom Wolfe described?
Is it a fit place to raise children?

There is no single answer to these questions, but the recession of the
early 1980s suggested to Nevadans one truism that they had previously
been loath to accept—and perhaps could not even later readily confess—
that they were the prisoners of the "industry" that they had tolerated. The
well-regulated servant had taken control of the lord and master; Caliban
had cast a spell over Prospero.

As I surveyed the comparative benefits and handicaps that Nevada
had received from its half-century encouragement of legalized gambling, I found little reason to join my fellow Nevadans in the traditional
chorus of self-congratulation. If we measure success in terms of dollars
or "improvements" on real estate, Nevada is, of course, one of the
leaders of the nation and the world. If, on the other hand, we evaluate the
state's performance on the basis of its service to its young people in the
classrooms, or the underprivileged, or the disabled, or the nation as a
whole, the record can hardly be a source of pride. Nevada was, at the

beginning of the 1980s, more parasitic than it had been in the days of the
mining and cattle frontiers, more dependent on federal largess than ever,
and less willing—if one judges from its social policies and budgeting
practices—to assume the normal obligations of a "sovereign" state in the
latter years of the twentieth century. There have been many analyses of
Nevada's record in welfare, human rights, and education in the past
three decades, and the overall conclusion is profoundly disturbing.

Welfare Policies

The most comprehensive mid-century indictment of Nevada's social
welfare policies came from the pen of Albert Deutsch and appeared in
the pages of *Collier's* in 1955.[1] After observing that Nevada was much
admired by outsiders for its favorable tax climate—it was commonly
known as the "taxpayers' paradise"—and that it had the third highest per
capita income among the American states, Deutsch catalogued the
evidence of the state's stinginess in the social and human services. It had
the highest crime rate and the highest suicide rate in the nation, but it had
no mental health clinics and only a single understaffed mental health
hospital. Its state prison and its orphans' home were badly overcrowded,
and its health and welfare services were at a primitive level, "below
those of many of the poorest states." Infant mortality rates and tuberculosis deaths were among the highest in the nation, and Nevada often tried
to transport its tuberculosis sufferers elsewhere for treatment. General
relief standards were among the worst in the country, Deutsch concluded after extensive interviews and research. Nevada received a
proportion of federal grants far higher than the national average, but in
general it did a poorer job of caring for the needy, and it was even
neglecting to take advantage of the federal aid that was available for the
families of dependent children. He concluded:

> And so goes the dismal story of Nevada's niggardliness. Too rich to
> accept normal taxes, too poor to maintain its institutions and agencies on a
> decent twentieth-century level, coddling known racketeers and making
> them respectable by legalizing their operations, while turning a cold
> poormaster's eye to its poor, its sick, its socially misshapen. . . .
>
> There are, of course, many good people in Nevada, concerned about the
> deplorable neglect of child and adult unfortunates, and wanting to do
> something about it. But they don't set the effective health and welfare
> policies of the gambling state, nor have they been able to modify it

much—as yet. An awakened citizenry will someday take into account the human costs of a gambling economy, and act on it, building up the vast potentials of this fabulously beautiful state.[2]

When Deutsch gathered his data, and in all the years since, the comparative statistics on crime and social problems were somewhat distorted against Nevada because of the fact that the state has had so many temporary residents—tourists or other transients who swell the demand for police and judicial services, social service agencies, and the like. Writers have often criticized Nevada for the amount of alcohol sold, disregarding the fact that much of it is consumed or carried away by the transients. But even allowing for the fact that the statistics on crime, welfare, and social practices are distorted by the unusual economy that has emerged, the consequences for the educational, social, and correctional institutions are no less serious. Nevadans generally are not more disposed toward antisocial behavior than their compatriots, but their favored "industry" almost certainly attracts social problems along with gamblers' money.

Deutsch wrote when the gambling boom was still young, before the prosperous days of the 1960s and 1970s; as we have seen, the imposition of a sales tax and the huge increases in gambling revenue were still to come. Did the increased revenue from those sources cause the problems that Deutsch mentioned to decline? A systematic, scholarly survey by a group of Nevadans, published in 1980 by the university's Bureau of Governmental Research, forces us to answer in the negative.

An excellent study by political scientist Elmer Rusco showed that for about twenty years before 1935, Nevada was one of the most generous states in the kind of "categorical" aid that it provided to needy mothers and children, to the elderly, and to the blind. It had a "pro-welfare stance," even though that was not a period of economic prosperity for the state.[3] Since the introduction of the New Deal programs for aid to the needy, however, Nevada's state-originated policies have been much less charitable; in fact, it has often been near the bottom of the list in terms of state expenditures for public welfare in times when the state treasury had bountiful budget surpluses. Although a smaller percentage of Nevada's residents were below the "poverty level" than the national average, the state government was obviously making less effort to help them than in most other states. While Nevada eventually joined in sharing the Aid to Families of Dependent Children program offered by the federal government, it administered the revenues in a most stringent manner, actually reducing the rolls of recipients during the 1970s, when the state's population—including the number of needy—was rising.[4] As a matter of fact, Nevada set its public policies toward welfare recipients so rigidly that it was often ranked among the poor southern states in terms of its expenditures for welfare, rather than among the states with high per capita incomes, whose prosperity it shared.

Rusco offered a number of hypotheses as possible explanations for the Nevada "anomaly" in welfare policy. He did not indicate which of these guesses he favored, if any, and he encouraged additional research on the subject. The combination of hypothetical answers, however, is worthy of additional emphasis. Perhaps, he conjectured, welfare attitudes had changed due to the population shift that had brought a higher percentage of Protestants of northern European origin to Nevada after the 1930s, as opposed to the pre-1935 period, when Nevada had a relatively larger share of residents of southern European and Catholic origin, who are presumed to be more favorable to public welfare. Perhaps also, according to one of his guesses, the high percentage of Mormons—who generally favor private and church assistance rather than governmental aid—has contributed to the change in attitude on welfare. In addition, the growth of the gambling business, which "encourages an extreme form of individualism" and "greater cynicism about the motives of other persons," might account for part of the "anti-welfare stance." And the fact that Nevada's labor unions and political parties have been weak—whereas such organizations are strong in some of the states that are both prosperous and pro-welfare—may be a factor. Nevada's poor have not had the class-based and labor-oriented organizations to represent them in Carson City.[5]

Not only was Nevada's government as unresponsive to welfare needs in the 1970s as it had been when Deutsch wrote his article in the 1950s, but other unfortunate social conditions that Deutsch mentioned in the Collier's article also persisted. Nevada still had, in the late 1970s, a suicide rate twice as high as the national average and substantially higher than that of other far western states. It had one of the highest rates of alcoholism, of murder/manslaughter, and of robbery, and the incidence of rape was about 60 percent higher than the national average.[6] Again, the large proportion of transients within Nevada may make these statistics somewhat unreliable as a basis for comparison, but Nevada could take little comfort from blaming the situation on the "outsiders" when it was paying the bills, or at least trying to pass them on to the federal government.

The prison population in Nevada, for example, has grown much more rapidly in the past few years than that in other states, not only because of the high crime rate but also because of the tendency of the criminal justice system to use incarceration as a form of punishment much more frequently than in most states. In spite of evidence that prison sentences usually do not rehabilitate convicts, early in the 1980s Nevada was leading its neighbors in expanding its prison system (the 1979 Nevada legislature appropriated money for 600 new cells) and in imposing long sentences and mandatory incarceration for some offenses. Charles Zeh, director of Washoe Legal Services, wrote in 1980:

> As long as we continue to build prisons, the will to treat the underlying problem, not the symptoms, will be lacking. The availability of additional cells reduces the pressures to find other, non-retributive, responses to the fundamental problems of society.[7]

Nevada had, as of 1980, one of the largest prison populations in the nation per 100,000 residents, and its detention facilities were dangerously overcrowded.

Civil Rights

There are many fields that Deutsch did not investigate that would have yielded additional information about the state government's neglect of basic human services. Nevada was slow to recognize and join the movement toward more equitable civil rights that transformed American history in the 1950s and early 1960s. Although the citizens of the state had not officially endorsed "jim crow" policies as some of the states of the Old South had done, they had quietly acquiesced in patterns of discrimination that effectively denied black citizens any places of opportunity or dignity in the trade unions or professions, had encouraged them to live in distinct regions of Reno and Las Vegas, and had denied them most places of public accommodation and entertainment. There were very few black lawyers, doctors, or professors; and while blacks were welcome as performers on the showroom stages of the hotel-casinos, they were not normally welcome as customers in the casinos and dining rooms. It was virtually impossible for a black person to get a job as a waiter, cook, or barber in Reno—although all of these fields were open to blacks in the South and East. Nevada's reputation in the 1950s as the "Mississippi of the West" was not totally deserved, because the state had no official policy of segregation in the schools and on the buses, and it took pride in the few black students (even those who were not athletes) at the university. But the image was not entirely undeserved, because of the *de facto* segregation in housing and the quiet discrimination in employment and in most places of public accommodation.

Until the early 1960s, official Nevada took almost no notice of the latent pattern of racial bigotry that it had inherited, partly because it seemed to be exempt from the growing tensions that were appearing in other parts of the country. As of 1960, there were still only about 13,500 blacks in the state, and more than 9,600 of them lived in Las Vegas. The first significant protest against racial discrimination occurred during the 1961 legislative session, when a few blacks conducted a "sit-in" in a segregated Reno hotel, picketed banks, and marched before the capitol building in Carson City. But as the Senate and Assembly had not yet been reapportioned to reflect the demographic changes, and only a handful of lawmakers in either house had an interest in human rights matters, the legislature took the path of least resistance.[8] It passed a token civil rights act, one of the last state lawmaking bodies outside the Deep South to make this gesture. The new law pronounced it to be the public policy of the state to foster the right of all people to have employment, housing, and services in places of public accommodation without discrimination on the basis of race, color, creed, or ancestry, and it created a five-member Commission on Equal Rights for the ostensible purpose of encouraging compliance with the policy.[9] Having done this, the legislature assured that the commission would be power-less to fulfill its mandate by providing it with no staff and almost no money. It had a budget of $2,500 per year to carry out its work.

But there was a growing conscience within the state and a growing awareness among blacks and reform-minded whites about the virtues of public discussion of this problem. In another of his informative scholar-ly studies, Elmer Rusco used the census statistics and the recent popula-tion projections, together with economic data, to show that blacks and Indians were not sharing in the general prosperity of the state. Both of the larger minority groups had higher unemployment rates, lower educa-tional levels, and poorer health than the population as a whole.[10] Rusco's work, completed in 1965, was the most revealing study of its kind during that decade, and it documented the growth of a pre-dominantly black "Westside" of Las Vegas at a rate much higher than that of the surrounding region and also showed a significant increase in the state's Indian population for the first time.

Although there were new social pressures on the national levels that well-informed Nevadans could not ignore, the state's institutions moved slowly. In 1964, the Nevada Equal Rights Commission, exercising its legal mandate to investigate reports of racial discrimination, used its subpoena powers to summon Lindsay Smith, an officer of a hotel-casino in Hawthorne, to a hearing. Smith's place of public accommodation had been flagrantly denying access to blacks. Instead of complying with the subpoena, Smith filed suit against the commission, asserting that it had no constitutional authority to enforce its subpoena and suing individual members for a quarter of a million dollars each for harassment. When a District Court judge in Reno granted his request for an injunction against the commission, it was paralyzed for several months. The attorney general's office, in the course of representing the commission and affirming its legal powers, concluded that the legislative authors of the Equal Rights statute had intentionally drafted an incomplete and weak statute to make it difficult for the commission to use its subpoena powers, The Supreme Court, nevertheless, ruled for the commission and affirmed its power to issue subpoenas and to take testimony in such cases. The civil rights movement thus won in the courts, in a decision written by Justice Gordon Thompson, a power that the legislature had only reluctantly initiated and had, in fact, tried to muzzle.[11]

The Nevada anti-discrimination law and the work of the Equal Rights Commission had little immediate effect on the racial barriers, but the passage of the federal Civil Rights Act of 1964 and a demonstration on the Las Vegas Strip had a profound result in one area—public accommodation. The 1964 Civil Rights Law, advocated by President Lyndon Johnson and enacted despite a Senate filibuster, was one of the most comprehensive in the history of the country, and it brought a number of changes in even the remotest part of the provincial South and West. The casino owners decided, virtually in concert, that it would be better to drop their barriers against blacks than to risk federal intervention, and their policies against nonwhite customers quietly disappeared. Most other businesses in the state followed suit without fanfare.

In the areas of equal employment and fair housing, the latent inequities continued. The Nevada legislature did not pass a Fair Housing Law until 1971—again lagging behind most other northern and western states. Organized resistance to such a law came from the real estate lobbies, but strong support from Governor O'Callaghan, an improved social attitude toward the rights of blacks, and a "majority of weak yesses" in the crucial committees of the legislature led to the eventual passage of a strong bill.[12] Another study by Rusco in 1973 on racial discrimination in employment showed that the existing federal and state laws as of that date still had not eliminated *de facto* bias of employers against blacks. Overall employment opportunities for blacks had not improved significantly in the Las Vegas casino industry between 1965 and 1971, Rusco found, and the federal civil rights agencies had been more diligent and effective in pressing for reform than the relatively weak Nevada Commission on Equal Rights. Blacks continued to be most heavily represented in the lowest-paying jobs and almost not at all in the professional, management, and technical positions.[13]

Even though the Nevada Equal Rights Commission had better funding and a professional staff by the end of the 1970s, it is questionable that it did much to alter the discrimination that existed in employment practices. It was still receiving many complaints in this field. Improvements in the law and in governmental authority to deal with discrimination hardly kept pace with the growth of the populations of minority groups. There were some 46,000 blacks in Las Vegas in 1980—10 percent of the population of the area. And it had virtually no effect on the quest for better social treatment of Indians, because it received very few complaints. The Native Americans of the state represented another dimension of the problem.

The Native Americans

In the years of the Great Depression, the Indians of Nevada fell into step with other Native Americans on the road to a fuller measure of self-determination. The policy that had been set in place by the Dawes Act of 1887—which had looked forward to the breaking up of the Indian reservations and the integrating of Indians more fully into the life of the majority culture—had been reversed by the Indian New Deal of the 1930s, and Nevada's larger Indian communities had reorganized themselves in response to the new national policy. Peoples who had long been regarded as wards of the government rather quickly demonstrated that within their ranks were some articulate, effective spokesmen who had adapted well to the challenge of citizenship.

The passage of the Indian Reorganization Act of 1934 stimulated a number of local organizing efforts in Nevada. The Pyramid Lake Paiutes, the Reno-Sparks Indian colony, and the Washo of Nevada and California were among the first of their race in the West to form legal tribes, approving formal constitutions in 1935. The Walker Lake Paiutes followed suit in 1937; before the end of the 1930s, a series of intertribal fairs, conferences, and alliances had been held.[14] In 1938, Dewey Sampson, a Northern Paiute, became the first Native American to be elected to the Nevada legislature, winning his seat in a district with a predominantly non-Indian population. In the same year, the Paiutes of Pyramid Lake on their own initiative took up a long-standing struggle to reclaim reservation lands on which "squatters" had been living for two generations. After a ten-year court battle, they won a settlement that evicted most of the non-Indians.[15]

Another segment of the Nevada Indian population that was affected by the Indian New Deal was the Te-Moak group of Western Shoshones. Although their ancestors had been removed from most of their lands in the 1860s and subjected to a long series of governmental efforts to restrict them to small reservations in the northeastern part of the state, they continued to regard themselves as a single people. This fact was partly recognized in 1938 when the Department of the Interior, an alert Indian superintendent named Alida Bowler, and leaders of the local Te-Moak bands cooperated to establish a constitution.

Although their predecessors had long been politically inactive, the Shoshones had a resource that now looms as a powerful weapon—an 1863 treaty negotiated between leaders of the Te-Moak bands and government agents of that era, who were presumably representing Abraham Lincoln. The treaty removed the bands from the land but did not specifically end their legal claims to the vast areas of the northern Great Basin where they had once roamed; in the 1970s, their lawyers pressed vigorously in the federal courts for the principle that their title to millions of acres had never been legally extinguished. Because the courts had held that, in a similar case in Maine, Indian tribes still had title to a large portion of that state that had since been transferred to private ownership, there was a clear possibility that the 2,000 Te-Moak Indians might have a strong constitutional claim to much of north-central and northeastern Nevada. The case was still pending in the higher courts in 1983. The Western Shoshones, incidentally, were one of the most effective groups in resisting the efforts of the Air Force to deploy the MX racetrack system in eastern Nevada in 1981.

There was little respite, however, in the century-old confrontation between the Indians and those whom they or their lawyers perceived as enemies. Financed in part by outside agencies such as the Ford Foundation, prompted and advised by innovative attorneys, Indians in Nevada—as elsewhere—reopened old legal and administrative disputes and tried to assert claims that had long since been dormant. One instance was the Truckee River water dispute (discussed in chapter 3), in which the

Pyramid Lake Paiutes intervened after the federal government had initiated the litigation. Another was the question of whether the Southern Pacific Transportation Company had a right to operate a branch line on the Walker River Indian Reservation, which it had done for seventy years without question; it was found by the courts to be "trespassing." On a dozen reservations an important commercial enterprise was the "smoke shop," where tribally sponsored merchants sold tobacco without collecting and paying the state tax, defying state law on the matter.

That the Indians were asserting their rights after a long period of quiescence was a healthy sign, even though it did cause some discomfort to the state government. The confrontation of the two cultures has never been easy in the western wilderness; the drunken Indian was always less acceptable under Anglo-Saxon law than the drunken cowboy or the miner who had "had a little too much." There is a built-in injustice that the conqueror inflicts upon the conquered; it has been so at least since the Romans imposed their particular blend of barbarism and culture on Gaul.

Perhaps there is no remedy for it this side of paradise, but America was, even if Nevada was not, the best place to try. The Indians have fought some vigorous legal battles here, with the aid of attorneys from the outside who did not always have all the facts or much of the law on their side.

One concept that the Indians' lawyers have brought to this latest confrontation is the idea that their aboriginal rights are the basis for restraining rampant commercialism, for slowing the process of land desecration that has occurred in recent times. The idea is that the Indians have, under the Winters reserved-right concept, the possibility of claiming waters for their reservation in a manner that will help save the environment not only within but also beyond the reservations, if their own life-patterns are thereby preserved. As one of the Native Americans' attorneys has written:

> The Winters doctrine can also be seen as a substantive National Environmental Policy Act insofar as it preserves and protects the reservations' environmental integrity. This has far-reaching implications. . . .
> The Winters doctrine is an extraordinarily powerful tool that does not require implementing legislation. It can be used to save vast areas of this land, particularly in the West, from environmental despoilation.[16]

It is an appealing doctrine, even though it did not succeed in one important attempt to invoke it in Nevada.[17] It hinted at one important line of defense that the constitutional system provided against the rape of the Great Basin, even when the state government would not assume its sovereign role to defend the land from the most reckless of the developers.

The trouble with the lawyers and the courts, helpful though they were, was that they were engaged in the "adversary" system; this encouraged confrontation and harassment, and this tendency was compounded by an aggressive press, which was far better at exploiting issues than at cultivating public discussion of them.

One can find indications of reawakened pride among the American Indians that did not involve confrontation and that did rise above the issue of whether a Paiute could sell tobacco on the reservation without sending a few pennies per package to Carson City. The most appealing example is that of the Las Vegas Paiute colony, located on twenty acres just a few blocks from the downtown casino center. On land that was deeded in 1911 by Helen Stewart, the pioneer matriarch of the old Las Vegas rancho, a few dozen Native American families persisted and clung to part of their Paiute-Shoshonean heritage in spite of the metropolis that engulfed them. They had no city water until 1962, although they were surrounded by the urban sprawl, and they had no constitution until 1970.[18] But the colony constituted in one of the gaudiest and least moral of American cities a level of conscience that could not easily be denied.

In the mid-1970s, almost exactly a hundred years after the Pyramid Lake and Walker River reservations had been recognized by a presidential executive order, two Native American residents of these communities published historical studies of them. These books were informative reflections on the ambiguities of the situation in which many Indians found themselves in the contemporary era. Nellie Shaw Harnar, a native of Wadsworth who spent much of her life on the Pyramid Lake Indian Reservation, produced a touching, sentimental account of her people's history that is faintly reminiscent of the writings of Sarah Winnemucca Hopkins, the "Paiute Princess" who had a significant reading audience in the late nineteenth century. Mrs. Harnar received her early education at the Stewart Indian School near Carson City, later studied in an Arizona university, and received her master of arts degree at the University of Nevada in Reno. She spent much of her life as a teacher and contributed to improved understanding between the Native American community from which she had come and the polyglot society of modern Nevada. Her book was written in a spirit of reconciliation.[19]

The second book, written by Edward Johnson of the Walker River Reservation, mirrors the mood of the discontented protesters of the recent era. His work combines industrious research with a litany of accusations against the "intruders," virtually all of whom are seen as enemies of "the People" (i.e., the Paiutes).[20] Johnson's commitment to political protest was typical of the attitude of the younger generation of Indians, to which Nevada's governing bodies had given little attention before the 1970s. Officially, Nevada's public institutions, with the occasional exception of its universities and public schools, have given little evidence of any sort of public conscience for the plight of this minority group, and Johnson's book is a response to that fact.

Despite all the ambiguities of the condition of the Nevada Indians, it was an encouraging fact that these people—whose ancestors had often been badly treated during the frontier and more recent periods of western history—had apparently been less tempted by the rampant, exploitive commercialism around them than most other social groups had. As of 1980, their numbers were increasing at the most rapid rate in history— from about 8,000 in 1970 to 13,300 in 1980—and this was most notable in rural areas. Although the costly litigation of recent years has produced little, they have won some concessions of land and water and have contributed a "still, small voice" to a public forum that apparently has had little social conscience.

Other Minorities

The Native Americans form the state's—as well as the nation's— oldest and most persistent challenge in interethnic relations; the arrival within our borders of tens of thousands of people of Hispanic origin during the past decade creates the newest, and it is difficult to find evidence that the governmental institutions have any disposition to regard them in any systematic way, although it should be evident that the tide of immigration from south of the border is just beginning to rise.

The 1980 census revealed that there were 53,879 people of "Spanish origin" in Nevada; ten years earlier there were not enough people in this category to be considered a significant minority group. But Nevada is on the fringe of the southwestern tier of states that have received most of the Mexican immigration, and Las Vegas is obviously a magnet for increasing numbers of Hispanics who want a quick taste of the materialism of American life.[21] Two-thirds of the Hispanic immigrants lived in Clark County; the vast majority of them were "urbanized," which often meant that they had taken jobs, when they were available, on the clean-up crews of the hotels and restaurants. Also, following the pattern that has become standard in other parts of the Southwest, several thousands had migrated northward into the potato fields and ranches in the northern part of the state. In 1980, more than 10 percent of the population of Elko, Humboldt, and Lander counties was classified as Hispanic.[22]

The most widely respected predictions and social indicators suggest that the influx of immigrants from the Latin countries is likely to continue and to accelerate in the years ahead, in view of Mexico's rapidly growing population. Nevada will almost certainly receive a significant number regardless of the fluctuations of the economy and the inconsistent efforts of the federal government to control the border crossings. If the response to human needs in this instance is no better than the state's past record in human services, the prospects for an enlightened program of ethnic assimilation are not bright.

There was, however, one good example from the past. Nevada once had a relatively large Chinese population; before the turn of the century, several communities had thriving "Chinatowns" that were part of the legacy of the era of railroad building in the bonanza days, and there is a record of a disgraceful pattern of persecution and discrimination against them.[23] In the first half of the twentieth century, the number of residents of Oriental descent had fallen to a very low level, but in recent years it has risen modestly. By 1980, the number of individuals whose ethnic background was Chinese, Japanese, Filipino, Vietnamese, or South Sea Islander was only about 13,000, so the influence of the Pacific Basin states east of the Sierra in this regard was minor. In general, these groups were concentrated in the urban centers, and they were totally integrated. Teachers and social workers often observed that the newer Oriental immigrants—the Vietnamese refugees, for example—were remarkably successful in making their way in the schools and professions. Apparently Nevada, like the West in general, has made genuine progress in its social attitudes toward this minority group.

The Equal Rights Amendment

The state's reputation as a socially retarded jurisdiction was underscored in the 1970s during the national confrontation over the proposed Equal Rights Amendment. When the constitutional amendment was proposed by Congress in 1971, a majority of the states ratified it quickly, but since a successful amendment must be approved by three-fourths of the states before it becomes part of the basic law of the land, the "unratified states" became the centers of the ideological struggle over whether women should have their fundamental rights affirmed in the Constitution. Nevada was one of the few "unratified states" outside the South, and its legislature indulged itself in a particularly messy and protracted struggle before it ultimately defeated the ERA.

The first resolution to approve the Equal Rights Amendment appeared in the Senate in 1973 and lost by a vote of 4 to 16. In 1975, it passed in the Assembly 27–13 but lost in the Senate 8–12. By this time thirty-four of the fifty states had ratified, and the debate in Nevada was particularly vitriolic. In 1977, after unseemly floor fights in which both the opponents of ERA and the lieutenant governor (who was president of the Senate and a supporter of ERA) engaged in bizarre parliamentary tactics to carry the day, the amendment appeared to win in the Senate on a tie-breaking procedural vote by the lieutenant governor, but it lost 15–24 in the Assembly. The legislature then, Pilate-like, washed its hands of the problem by referring it to the electorate, which voted by a two-to-one margin against the amendment. Thus Nevada demonstrated once again, and emphatically, that its popular will was much more hostile to the equal rights concept than was the case in most of the other northern and western states.

It was obvious that in Nevada, as in much of the rest of the nation, women had an important role in defeating the Equal Rights Amendment. As a perceptive article in *Harper's* magazine demonstrated, women's groups played a decisive role in arousing fears and suspicions over what was essentially a simple and straightforward effort to assure women equal status under the law.[24] Some of the strongest opponents of ERA were the women. It was also evident that a strong alliance of business groups—"an invisible lobby of business" as it came to be called—withheld its support in the pivotal states at crucial times. In Nevada, where the tourist-oriented businesses—including the gambling businesses—exercise an unusually large influence on a small legislature, the basic attitude was against ERA. Conservative church groups, especially the Latter-day Saints, manifested their opposition to ERA in the 1978 referendum.

Public Education

Perhaps the most accurate measure of how well Nevada's peculiar economy has served the state is a survey of its educational system. How have the public schools and the institutions of higher learning fared in the interval between the Depression of the 1930s and the recession of the 1980s? In general, the conclusion must be the same as it was for the social welfare programs, with some minor modifications.

In the 1940–1941 school year, the net enrollment in all of Nevada's primary, secondary, and kindergarten classes was 21,695—slightly less than 20 percent of the population of the state. A large percentage of these pupils were in the widely scattered rural school districts with inadequate buildings and minimal facilities—accommodations inherited in many cases from pioneer days. The one-room school was still standard in many places.[25] At the state's only university, which was located in Reno, there were about 1,000 regular students pursuing degrees through a curriculum that had been little changed since the turn of the century.

In 1980, Nevada had 145,000 pupils in the public schools and about 40,000 in its two universities and five community colleges. The physical facilities were much better, and the educational opportunities for young people were incomparably more varied, but there was still strong evidence of official neglect of fundamental educational principles.

Consider first the evolution of the public school system. The original program for organizing public education, established in the 1860s and still in effect in the 1950s, left most of the responsibility for financing the primary and secondary schools at the local level. There were more than 200 local school districts, each managed by a separate school board and dependent primarily on the property taxes assessed and collected in the district. The school board selected and paid the teachers and set the curriculum within some general guidelines established at the state level. Some school districts were obviously very poor; a few were quite wealthy because they had a strong property tax base. Many schools in Reno and Las Vegas were becoming severely overcrowded in the early 1950s because of the population growth, compounded by the arrival in the classrooms of the postwar "baby boom."

By 1954, the situation had become so serious that Governor Charles Russell called a special session of the legislature, which financed a study of the state's educational needs. The George Peabody College for Teachers, a Tennessee institution, conducted a survey and provided the recommendations for an overhaul of both the school system and the method of financing it—a reform package that was enacted into law in the 1955 legislature. The Peabody study showed, in findings that complemented those of the Deutsch article in *Collier's,* that, although Nevada was one of the wealthiest states in the West in per capita income, it was making a poor showing in public school expenditures per student, and there were great inequities in the amount of money available to the various school districts. It also showed that Nevada was getting a greater percentage of its school revenues from federal sources than most of the other western states were.[26] It was the familiar story; the state that had taken pride in being the "storm shelter for the tax weary" during the Depression had not been willing to adopt any of the so-called nuisance taxes—on retail sales, income, or inheritance—that were part of the revenue-producing sources for most other states. And its property taxes were low in most areas, not only because there was a constitutional limit but also because assessments on real property were far below market value.

Led by Governor Charles Russell and Assembly Speaker Cyril Bastian of Caliente, the 1955 legislature approved not only the Peabody school reform plan but also financial means of implementing it. For the first time in the state's history, the lawmakers enacted a 2 percent tax on retail sales.

The Peabody plan called for the consolidation of the scores of tiny, isolated school districts into seventeen countywide districts and proposed a formula for equalizing the resources of the richer and the poorer districts. It was a complex formula, calculating the needs of each district according to the number of students, the number of teachers, and certain other variables, and then financing them partly through a mandatory local property tax of seventy cents per year on each $100 of assessed valuation and partly through allotments from a State Distributive School Fund, which got much of its revenue ultimately from the sales tax. Since there was pressure to leave some autonomy at the local level as well as to standardize the financing, the legislature left the local school districts the authority to impose a property tax of eighty cents per year on each $100 of assessed valuation, so in the end the disparity between rich and poor districts remained. Yet the Peabody plan did enable Nevada to do much better for its schools as a whole; by 1960, Nevada was ninth in the nation in the level of its expenditures per pupil in the public schools.[27] And because of the willingness to approve bond issues for new buildings, the physical facilities of the schools improved considerably in the 1960s.

In 1967, the legislature altered the Peabody plan by adopting the "Nevada Plan," which involved an additional tax of 1 percent on all retail sales, known as the Local School Support Tax. The main features of the Peabody formula for determining the needs of the school districts remained in effect, but this was often less than the schools needed to keep pace with the rapid population growth that occurred in the larger cities. Nevada was about at the national average in terms of its pupil-teacher ratio in 1960 (23.6 students per teacher), and the state retained its relatively favorable position for about a decade. Then, almost imperceptibly, it began to slip downward in comparisons with the national and regional averages.

During the administration of Governor Mike O'Callaghan (1971–1978), the growth of the public school system paralleled the rise in the state's population, and O'Callaghan, himself a former teacher, was sympathetic to the requests of the school interests. He was a fiscal conservative; in his first message to the legislature in 1971, he affirmed the traditional Nevada attitude, which was highly popular and clearly matched the mood of most of the taxpayers:

> We are at a point in time when we must face some hard realities concerning the financial condition of our State. The problems are complex, but our available alternatives in meeting those problems are relatively simple.
>
> We may raise taxes to finance new programs and more generously endow our present programs.
>
> Or we may resolve to operate within our existing tax framework, thus requiring a careful system of priorities.
>
> I am committed to the second course of action.[28]

Such an approach was, of course, readily endorsed by the legislature, not only in 1971 but in the next three succeeding legislative sessions of O'Callaghan's term. Cautious administration and steadily rising revenues from the gambling and sales taxes provided the state treasury with its best balances ever. In his last message to the legislature in 1977, O'Callaghan proposed a budget in which 45 percent of the general fund revenues were to be derived from the taxes and fees imposed on the gambling housees and related entertainment taxes.[29]

That Nevada might be putting itself into a vulnerable financial position by becoming increasingly dependent on gambling taxes, and on the sales, cigarette, and liquor taxes that were to a large extent paid by the tourists, was well known to the best budget analysts, but there were no important voices raised for diversifying the tax base. It was widely assumed—and no doubt the assumption was correct—that the electorate would not tolerate it. Nevada was by this time one of only three states that had neither a corporate nor a personal income tax. It was the only state without an inheritance tax, which in effect gave the federal government a larger share of tax revenue from large estates probated in Nevada than in any other state.

In the meantime, by the end of the 1970s, educational statistics reminiscent of those that existed in the days before the Peabody reform began to appear. In 1977–1978, Nevada had the second-highest per capita income in the nation—$8,276 as compared with a national average of $7,043. Yet it was forty-eighth among the fifty states in the percentage of per capita income spent directly for education.[30] It was also evident that Nevada had a significant "out-migration" of its young people to other states for college-level training, so that it was in effect assuming less of the cost of higher education than most states.[31]

If the political leaders at the end of the 1970s had followed the example of their predecessors of the 1950s, they might have found new sources of revenue in some of the forms of taxation that were in use in other states or in higher levels for some of the existing taxes—for Nevada's property taxes and sales taxes were still low when compared with those of most neighboring states. But the decision makers of the more recent period were not of the same mettle as those of the previous generation, and their political lives were complicated by the fact that a taxpayers' rebellion broke out in California and frightened the wits out of fiscal planners on the eastern slopes of the Sierra Nevada. California's famous Proposition 13, the constitutional amendment that drastically reduced property taxes by initiative petition and largely tied the hands of the legislators of that state on other tax matters, had a counterpart in Nevada known as Proposition 6. When this matter appeared on the ballot in November of 1978, the voters approved it overwhelmingly and caused panic in Carson City.

Because the Nevada Constitution, unlike that in California, does not allow an initiative proposition to become part of the Constitution on the basis of only one popular vote, the Nevada budget makers had time to propose an alternative taxing and budgeting formula. The 1979 legislature responded to the "taxpayers' rebellion" by reducing real property taxes by about 27 percent, removing the sales tax on food, exempting household goods from property taxation, and placing a "ceiling" on certain state and local governmental expenditures. When this proposal was offered to the voters in 1980 in lieu of Proposition 6, the majority of them accepted it and rejected Proposition 6. To replace the revenue that had been lost by the tax reductions, the 1981 legislature increased taxes on retail sales from 3 percent (or in some counties from $3\frac{1}{2}$ percent) to $5\frac{3}{4}$ percent, with the expectation that a large percentage of this increase would be borne by the tourists. It appeared that the legislature had once again found a way to get the visitors to pay more of the state's governmental and educational costs, while making matters easier for the locals. When Governor List spoke to the Carson City Rotary Club, he referred proudly to the fact that Nevada had "the best tax climate in the country," with no corporate or personal income tax, no franchise, inheritance, or inventory tax, one of the lowest property tax rates in the country, and—even with the increase in sales taxes—a lower sales tax than most other states.[32]

But then came the recession/depression of 1981–1982, and the entire arrangement backfired. By sharply reducing the property tax, Governor List's program had undermined a fundamental part of the financing base for the school districts. The schools had been required to surrender much of their traditional property tax support with the assurance that the difference would be provided from the state treasury. This seemed to work well in the short run, but when the 1982 sales tax collections fell far below expected levels, and when gambling revenues failed to rise as they had done each year for three decades, the state treasury found itself not with an anticipated surplus of $33 million but with a $70 million deficit. Nevada's government—and especially its most costly segment, the educational system—was poorly prepared for this eventuality; it could no longer fall back on property taxes. And because of the revenue shortage, the educational institutions fared badly again in the 1983 legislative session.

Higher Education

Frederick Rudolph, one of the finest historians of higher education in the United States, has described well the rise of the great American universities from the foundations of the small colleges between about 1880 and 1940.[33] The course offerings, the faculty research, and the public service activities of the institutions of higher learning expanded considerably in many parts of the country, and enrollment grew four or five times faster than the population. This was not so in Nevada in the years before and immediately after the Second World War; in the field of higher education, the state was even more primitive—by comparison with other states—than it was in the field of social welfare.

Like the other western states, Nevada had established a land-grant college soon after its admission to the Union, in order to get the benefits of the Morrill Act of 1862, which provided land grants for the support of higher education. The little institution that had been founded in Elko in 1874 and moved to Reno in 1886 was called a university, but for more than a half-century only a handful of its faculty performed the kind of scholarly research and public service that is normally associated with such an institution in the twentieth century.

In 1941, the university was located on an 86-acre campus at the north edge of Reno; it had a faculty of about 100 to serve its 1,000 students. (A student-faculty ratio of 10-to-1 seemed almost utopian in the early 1980s, after a series of miserly gubernatorial and legislative budgets had forced a ratio of approximately 22-to-1 on the university and an even higher ratio on the community colleges.) At the 1941 commencement ceremonies—the fiftieth to be held in Reno—about 200 degrees or diplomas were awarded, including 7 master's degrees and 16 two-year normal school diplomas.[34] The "university" was still a tiny provincial college serving almost exclusively the in-state population with traditional undergraduate arts and science classes. It was also training a few mining, engineering, and agricultural specialists in the tradition of the land grant provisions of the Morrill Act. The majority of its graduates were liberal arts students.

The concept of the university as the creator and arbiter of knowledge, as an institution dedicated to the advancement of research as well as to teaching, was understood by at least part of the faculty, but this idea had only faintly begun to dawn upon the people of the state. The Nevada Bureau of Mines, as an adjunct of the School of Mines, and the Experiment Station and Extension Service of the College of Agriculture had extensive reputations for publications relating to mineral industries, ranching, and livestock raising; this was of course comprehensible to the Nevada electorate. Only three or four individuals on the faculty were doing research in the arts and sciences that received any scholarly attention outside the state. The president of the university, Leon Hartman, took pride in operating the university in the most stringent manner possible, and he liked to return surplus money to the state treasury. A legislative investigating committee of 1939 directed criticism at even the small amount of research that was underway. Insofar as these activities reflected the mood of the citizens of Nevada, the people of the state were content with a small community college.

For two decades before 1939, the state had appropriated no money for new buildings; the university was functioning with facilities and equipment that were at least a quarter-century old and had been poorly maintained. In 1939 and 1941, the legislature appropriated the first money in two decades for new buildings, and it reflected priorities by spending $175,000 for a new engineering building and $300,000—an unprecedented sum—for a new gymnasium. During the war, when regular enrollments were low, the faculty assumed responsibility for training military personnel who were stationed nearby; at the end of the war, it acquired surplus army metal Quonset buildings to house the departments of English and art, where they remained in "temporary" quarters for decades. If one made a judgment about Nevada's attitudes toward the arts and letters from the state of their housing accommodations at the university, it would have been appropriate to conclude that they were not yet in high esteem in this corner of the frontier.

Through the end of the 1940s and into the early 1950s, while institutions of higher learning in most neighboring states were enjoying the fruits of prosperity, the Nevada university continued to function on its Depression-oriented tax base, with classrooms crowded by returning war veterans, a faculty paid at disgracefully low levels, and very modest research expectations.

The University of Nevada began to widen the scope of its services to the state and to expand its research role in a number of academic and professional fields in the middle 1950s. This involved not only the introduction of permanent extension courses and, in 1957, a branch campus in Las Vegas, but also the active recruitment of faculty members who had records and promise of productivity in research specialties as well as in teaching. These developments coincided with the administration of President Minard W. Stout (1952–1957), who was, ironically, the most controversial chief executive in the century-long history of the institution. While Stout did much to make the state aware of how badly it had neglected its university, he also adopted authoritarian tactics that proved to be painfully disruptive to some of the academic programs and brought national censure down upon himself and the board of regents.[35] He was ultimately fired by the board after the legislature had intervened to enlarge its membership.

One of the many ironies of the Stout years was that even as he began to try to expand the financial base of the university, he and the regents undertook to dismiss some of the faculty members whom they regarded as "troublemakers," men who incidentally were among the few highly regarded research scholars on the faculty. Two of these men were biologists and three were English professors with excellent research and teaching records to their credit; they were precisely the kind of academicians who could bring distinction to a developing university and provide excellent pedagogical training to its students. Court rulings ultimately forced Stout and the regents to retreat from their policy of purging some of the university's best scholars, but the controversy that followed this episode troubled the institution for five years. Had Stout not begun his presidency with procedures that created a climate of mistrust and brought national censure, he might have had one of the most productive administrations in the history of the university, because there was a more

obvious base of public and financial support than ever before in the
state's history. During the middle 1950s, as we have seen earlier, the
enactment of a retail sales tax and an increase in the gambling taxes had
markedly improved the revenue situation in Carson City.

For a dozen years after Stout's departure, the university prospered as
never before, because the legislature did much to correct the pattern of
benign neglect that had prevailed since the earliest years of statehood.
Not only did the Las Vegas campus become a center of learning,
recruiting an aggressive young faculty with much promise for scientific,
humanistic, and professional contributions to the wider world, but the
university also established a Desert Research Institute for scientific
study in 1959 and a community college division beginning in 1967. The
Reno campus was able to expand its professional offerings beyond the
traditional arts-and-sciences, mining-engineering, and agricultural
areas into new fields of business, nursing, medicine, and other specialties not previously taught in Nevada. Las Vegas faculty members
quickly established themselves regionally and nationally in such dis-
ciplines as hotel management, theater arts, anthropology, biology, and
radiology, among others. Doctoral programs were established in several
departments on the Reno campus, and many Nevada professors com-
peted successfully for financial grants from federal and private sources
to assist them in their investigations. Not only did scores of faculty
members publish their books and articles with national and international
presses, but the University of Nevada Press gained recognition as a
publisher of high-quality books and artistic reprints on western subjects.
In terms of public support for higher education, Nevada compared
favorably with other western states in the period from 1957 to 1971,
during the administrations of governors Grant Sawyer and Paul Laxalt.

By the time of its centennial observation in 1974, it appeared that the
university system had come of age. It was serving more than 20,000
students throughout the state—more than ten times as many as had been
accommodated on the Reno campus only a quarter-century before. But a
few years earlier, a subtle change had been made in the method of
financing the university system that ultimately did much to damage the
four-year institutions.

In 1969, the legislature adopted a formula for funding the various
units of the university on a "full-time equivalent" basis, providing that
there should eventually be a student-faculty ratio of 20-to-1. Although
the national norm for universities was approximately 16-to-1, and even
though repeated studies showed that 20-to-1 was abnormal for an
institution that was offering advanced degrees to a high percentage of its

students, this formula became the foundation for financing higher education in subsequent sessions of the legislature. While it was initially assumed that the universities in Reno and Las Vegas could move toward the 20-to-1 goal over a decade—finally reaching that level in 1980, Governor O'Callaghan decided in 1971 to accelerate the process and to impose the new ratio immediately, and the legislature acquiesced. As a result, the two universities operated during the 1970s with a much more restricted funding formula than they had known in the previous decade. On the whole, the universities were able to pay their professors at a level comparable with the national averages, but because of the "numbers game," it forced unprofessional demands on them in trying to maintain the broad programs that had been approved in the 1960s and in trying to deal with the numbers of students who were arriving.

Although the universities in Las Vegas and Reno had common financial problems in the later 1970s, they affected the two institutions differently. Because Las Vegas grew much more rapidly, UNLV served a total student population of approximately 6,500 in the fall of 1973 and about 11,450 nine years later. On the Reno campus, the head count showed about 7,100 in the fall of 1973 and nearly 9,600 in the fall of 1982. UNLV was able to add many more younger faculty members and therefore introduced new fields of specialization, but the student-teacher ratio remained shockingly high for an American institution of higher learning. UNR, with less growth and an older faculty, was also more heavily committed to costly professional programs in agriculture, mining, medicine, and engineering, and it had fewer options for innovation.

It was almost as though these institutions were in a "third world" country, where it is not uncommon to establish an institution that is given the name "university" and then denied the resources to do the work required.

When Governor List assumed office in 1979, he tried to move the universities to a 22-to-1 ratio in yet another "economy" measure. In presenting his first budget, he read the national population statistics in such a way that he anticipated a decline in the enrollments in higher education and proposed that during the 1979–1981 biennium the size of the UNR faculty be reduced by forty-two full-time equivalent positions and that UNLV lose twenty-one full-time equivalent positions.[36] In practice, it was a formula for erasing many of the gains that the university had made during the 1960s. (Ironically, at the same time that Governor List was proposing to cut the university faculties by sixty-three positions, he recommended the addition of eighty-seven new positions to the Gaming Control Board staff.) List was wrong in his enrollment projections, as he was on the financial projections; student registrations continued to rise at both universities and at the community colleges, and rising costs greatly exceeded the available funding.

The university and the regents were ultimately able to avoid such drastic cuts, but the legislatures of 1979 and 1981—even before the onset of the recession/depression of 1981–1982—took a much harder line on university budgeting than they had done since the 1940s. There was an effort by several legislators to force the universities to reduce their research and to require the faculties to assume even larger teaching duties. One result was that when outside scholars visited the Reno campus in 1982 to conduct graduate program reviews and evaluations, they were amazed at the heavy teaching loads that were expected of Nevada faculties, and they uniformly recommended more emphasis on research. On the other hand, the visiting scholars were often impressed by the excellent physical plants that the state had provided for its faculties and students.

At the level of higher education, as in the public school system, a deceptive sense of progress was stimulated during the 1970s because many impressive new "capital improvements" for colleges and universities appeared upon the horizon in the Great Basin and the Las Vegas Valley. During the 1970s, about $40 million worth of new buildings arose on the main Reno and Las Vegas campuses and for the community colleges in Carson City, North Las Vegas, Henderson, and Reno. The Desert Research Institute enlarged its plant as well, and the Medical School expanded to encompass three buildings on the north edge of the Reno campus.

Much of this new construction became possible because of the enactment in 1971 of the Higher Education Capital Improvements Fund, which received $5 million annually from a federal rebate. This money came from a federal tax upon Nevada slot machines and had previously gone into the national treasury; 80 percent of this money that was being collected in Nevada was to be returned to the state to finance new buildings and equipment for higher education. This was a windfall, and the history of inferior and antiquated buildings that had retarded the institutions of higher education for decades was interrupted. At long last, visitors to the campus could admire the quarters and the equipment that Nevada—or rather the patrons of the slot machines—had provided to the faculties and students.

The catch was that the fund that allowed the construction and the initial equipping of these buildings did not provide for their maintenance, and in general money from this fund was not available to pay utility costs or for the replacement of outmoded equipment. As a result, the universities and colleges found themselves rich in real estate and "improvements," but badly in need of new operating money, which the legislature continued to provide in the old, niggardly amounts. It was possible to get fancy new typewriters, but hard to get books for the libraries. Rising utility and maintenance costs in the 1970s crippled the general budgets and forced the campuses in the northern part of the state to adjust their winter operations to try to save fuel. This was nothing especially new, as universities throughout the western world had been doing that for centuries, but it also provided a rationale in Nevada to reduce academic programs.

The legislatures of 1979 and 1981 added the garnish to this setting when another windfall came from Washington—an additional rebate of the other 20 percent of the slot machine taxes collected in Nevada. The legislation that produced this bonanza was enacted in response to strong pressures from the athletic boosters, and on the strength of this activity the legislature authorized bonds for the building of two large pavilions— one on the Las Vegas campus at a cost of $30 million and one on the Reno campus for which $26 million was authorized. This was not money that the state had in the treasury; most of it was to come from bonds financed by the Higher Education Capital Improvements Fund. Nevada was, once again, "betting on the come line," putting itself into debt in anticipation of big gambling revenues in the future. It was Monopoly, or Break-the-Bank, or Beat the Dealer on a grand scale.

In brief, the sports pavilions were not financed on a "pay-as-you-go" basis, as had generally been the case with construction in the 1970s. In this instance, the legislature was committing the anticipated income from slot machine revenue—from the second windfall—for many years in advance to pay the cost of construction and the principal and interest on the bonds. In one gesture the legislature, with the acquiescence of the universities' leaders, had not only committed more money to the erec- tion of its huge sports arenas—which were called for public relations reasons "multi-purpose" pavilions—than to most other academic and research programs in the university system in the previous decade, but it had also created substantial fiscal risks for the future. One of the difficult problems of the regents and the legislature in the early 1980s was finding a way to pay for the operation of the pavilions indirectly from the slot machine tax rebate money without further complicating the universities' fiscal situation. In spite of the near-desperate financial condition that had forced the universities to cut their library budgets and to cancel some graduate programs in foreign languages and philosophy, and to reduce the mathematics offerings, it seemed urgent, in 1984, to find money for the operation of the pavilions. And the university officers found it, even as they were cutting the budgets for learning.

By the middle of the 1980s, there was the hope—optimists said there was the probability—that the pavilions would "pay their own way" from the revenues they produced, and there would be no need for outside subsidies. Whether this would prove to be true over the long term was an open question.

The situation was a metaphor for the Nevada of the 1980s. The state had committed itself so completely to the tourist and entertainment industry that its political and professional leaders had come to establish most of their priorities on what would serve the tourist economy. The $56-million sports pavilions were symbols of the Nevada aspirations of the 1980s, as Boulder Dam had been the symbol for the 1930s.

And so we Nevadans have, in these forty years, created an Alice in Wonderland kingdom for the delight and confusion of those who venture into our realm. We have spent many of our spiritual and natural resources playing Tweedledum and Tweedledee, and we have paid all homage to the Queen of Hearts. But we have paid little mind to the worlds that may lie beyond our political borders, and we have assumed very little of the responsibility that America requires in this century of challenge. For all its so-called cosmopolitanism, Nevada remains, at heart, a parasite and a provincial backwater, contributing little of its social or material energy to the problems of war and peace, human rights, or protection of the environment. It has submerged its social conscience and sense of duty to the effort to keep the gambling business, and the fantasy that surrounds it, "healthy."

CHAPTER 7

A FIFTH NEVADA: WITH A CONSCIENCE?

IN THE PRECEDING two chapters, I suggested emphatically that this has become "a state without a conscience," and certainly the record of the political entity that operates under the name "Nevada" has a record that invites that indictment. Yet, as Deutsch recognized three decades ago and as anyone who has got beyond the casinos and the fast-buck artists around them must know, there is indeed a Nevada of charitable, compassionate citizens who want social justice for all and better educational institutions for their children. They have not, however, been heard from on many issues for many seasons.

Nevada might best be compared to a healthy human who has been well fed, well housed, and well clothed for many years, but who is, as a matter of fact, somewhat overweight and emotionally unstable. He has been overindulgent; he has committed himself to too many of the frills over the years, and has neglected to plan for the future.

Or is it rather that Nevada has allowed itself to become a kind of institutional Howard Hughes, self-imprisoned by the darkness of the gambling economy that has become its fixation, afraid of the outside world and content to live by its own cloistered and distorted values? Is Nevada the victim of a self-induced neurosis that it is unable to treat without help?

In my more pessimistic moments, I have felt that the latter is the case; probably the actual situation is halfway between these two conditions.

Nevada often seems to be a sick society, having got sicker as it got richer, and more disposed to neglect the humane values as it became more preoccupied with the millions and billions that it has taken in from the tourists. I have a few suggestions. The first is that the federal government should intervene immediately to assume responsibility for cleaning house in the gambling industry.[1] Nevada has demonstrated that it cannot overcome this addiction on its own; it is a user that cannot manage its own treatment, and it is in the business of pushing its skills elsewhere, to the detriment of the nation. The FBI, IRS, and all the other federal agencies with authority to do so should pursue their work with diligence—and by all means consistently with the Bill of Rights and the established procedures of law—within Nevada and elsewhere. The "sting" operations that captured certain state senators and county officers in the abuse of their public trusts should continue at an accelerated pace.

But we must not rely upon the "feds" alone; we have done that too often in the past, when, like other addicts, we have wanted a quick fix. What is needed is the emergence of a "fifth Nevada," created in part from the elements of the four subdivisions identified in the first two chapters and in part from the groups that have arisen in response to the problems discussed in the preceding three chapters. I have in mind a new Sagebrush Alliance, like the one that emerged *ad hoc* in response to the threat of the MX racetrack deployment. Note that we are focusing here on the Sagebrush Alliance, a broad cross section of Nevada citizens interested in preserving the admirable parts of the state's heritage and resources—not the Sagebrush Rebellion—which was essentially only a combination of livestock owners and opportunist politicians who raised a small whirlwind and accomplished nothing.

An Agenda for the Sagebrush Alliance

One of the first items on the agenda would be an effort to control the gambling business that in recent years has been out of control, as regards both its growth and its operation. In view of the record of the last forty years, it is evident that Nevada's government, although run by people who are, most of the time, honest and conscientious, will not be able on its own to purge the criminal element from gambling. That is why we need help—immediately and desperately. The new Sagebrush Alliance should affirm that Nevada has failed to purge its "industry" of the criminal element, or—if it has been able to do so for brief periods—it has been unable to keep the professional racketeers out. In order to show its determination to keep the criminals from siphoning any more dollars through Nevada into the coffers of crime, the state should immediately commit itself to full cooperation with the anti-crime task forces, with the Federal Bureau of Investigation, and with the Internal Revenue Service. The alliance should insist that the governor, appointees, senators and representatives in Congress, and all others in high political office cease their obstructionist strategies and make their highest priority not the defense of the state's prerogatives in an industry riddled with disease, but therapy that is both drastic and thorough. They should announce that a cleaner "industry" is preferable, even if it is smaller, to one that is subsidizing organized crime, and they should act upon that principle.

The alliance should also advocate a moratorium—perhaps for five years or so—on the authorization of new casinos or gambling enterprises of any kind. Recognizing that Nevada already has too much of its economic life tied to the vagaries of a single "industry"—as it did in the days when mining was its almost exclusive source of prosperity—it should announce that it will not allow any more of the state's land, water, or other resources to be committed to the use of the casino, or casino-related businesses, before the end of the decade, at the earliest. It should also demand that if and when any gambling license is revoked because of demonstrated criminal activity or connections, the casino affected will remain closed at least through the end of the moratorium, despite the losses that will have to be sustained by the state treasury and the employees.

Such a policy could demonstrate to potential nongambling industry investors that Nevada truly is interested in diversifying its economy—an objective often proclaimed but then repeatedly undercut by the un-controlled expansion of the casinos. Such a policy might be welcomed by the casino operators who are managing their businesses in an honest way. The state legislature and agencies would then have to conduct their business on the assumption that the gambling-tourist taxes are not going to pay an ever-growing share of the bills, and that other forms of revenue should be considered.

The period of the moratorium would provide an opportunity to con-sider many options, including the long-range reduction of the gambling business.

Nourishing the Starved Institutions

The Sagebrush Alliance, if it were composed of people of conscience like the majority of those who served on the MX environmental impact review teams, might wish to make or to promote a review of the state's fiscal and taxation structure, similar to the one made by the Peabody College thirty years ago. Such a study would entertain the possibility of new taxes, even in such sacred-cow areas as income and inheritance taxation, if such were necessary to give Nevada's impoverished institutions the kind of fiscal support they need to raise them from the lowest levels of funding in the nation.

Such a review and reform of the tax structure is unlikely to begin in the legislature or in the governor's office, staffed as those institutions usually are by politically ambitious, less-than-courageous individuals, most of whom have been elected with the help of substantial campaign contributions from the casinos. The legislature of Nevada meets only once every two years under normal circumstances, and then for far too short a time and under too many pressures to undertake any meaningful review. But perhaps if a broad cross section of citizens, concerned not merely with the state's "image" but mainly with its integrity, were to take the initiative, the governor and the legislature could be made to react responsibly, as they did in the 1950s when Nevada faced a crisis in its institutional life.

Who Are the Potential Members of the Sagebrush Alliance?

Perhaps the elements of the fifth Nevada—the Nevada of conscience—existed at the beginning of the 1980s, but only in latent form. Perhaps it consists of some of the elements that came together for a few weeks while the Air Force's MX racetrack environmental statement was under review. Perhaps at least some representatives of the ranching interests of the Humboldt region, some voices from the mining industry and the region where it once flourished, and some speakers for the Indians, the environmentalists, the scholars, and the moralists could find a common cause in trying to preserve what is left of the Nevada heritage from the insatiable appetite of the gambling economy. For all their differences, perhaps they could be persuaded that they have a mutual interest in controlling the "industry" that their political leaders have failed to police effectively, for the sake of the nation as a whole as well as for the Nevada they all admire.

Let us identify some of the potential allies in enterprise; none of them is entirely free from the dependency that the state now has on the gambling economy, but some of them have ethical resources that they have allowed to remain dormant in the face of the evidence that has been summarized above.

The Churches

The churches of Nevada have been strangely silent on the question of the state's subservience to a gambling economy that has been shown repeatedly to be riddled with criminal influences. Perhaps there is no better evidence than this that the entire society of Nevada has become so dependent on the business that it has acquiesced in the parasitical relationship that has developed with the "industry." A number of the churches have taken the position that there is nothing inherently evil in gambling, and therefore its legality is not to be questioned. It seems often to follow from this position that, like Pontius Pilate, the religious institutions can wash their hands of any responsibility for the social consequences.

Billy Graham and other evangelical preachers have had their days in Las Vegas, have deplored the obvious vices of society there as elsewhere, and have left with their net worth none the worse for the visit. It would seem to be enough to have improved the chances for a few wayward souls to achieve salvation; the need for social improvement is recognized, but no practical action—unless prayer and intellectual surrender to Christ be so regarded—is advocated. Thus the solution to our problems lies in heaven, or so it would seem.

The Catholic church, by far the largest in terms of its declared adherents, has likewise been a nonentity in terms of any moral force for the control of the social evils surrounding the casinos. *The New Catholic Encyclopedia* asserts that "gambling, though a luxury, is not considered sinful except when the indulgence in it is inconsistent with duty."[2] This seems to be a mandate to condone participation in the business either as operator or as sucker at the tables and machines, without regard for the social evils that arise from it. Yet the same summation adds:

> Because gambling can become a major social evil, most societies have laws restricting, controlling, or prohibiting certain forms of it. Generally speaking, the laws appear to be just, and defiance of them on a large or professional scale seems incompatible with Christian morality.[3]

It should be evident to the clergy of this denomination that there is indeed a question of Christian morality to be considered in this instance.

One of the most potentially formidable moral forces in the state in the 1980s is the Mormon church. This was not so at the beginning of the 1940s, when its presence was felt almost not at all in state politics.

In 1942, Wallace Stegner published his *Mormon Country,* a thoughtful, lyrical interpretation of Utah and the adjacent areas where the life-style of the Latter-day Saints was the predominant cultural form. It is still a splendid book, a useful tool for analyzing one of the important influences on the Nevada of the 1980s.[4]

The western boundary of the Mormon country, Stegner said, was difficult to identify. The Mormons once claimed all of the Great Basin and the lower Colorado River for their state of Deseret. They made their first permanent settlements in Nevada along the eastern slope of the Sierra in 1851 and in the Las Vegas Valley in 1855 in a effort to establish their jurisdiction; had they not been frightened by the threat of a federal army marching upon them from the east in 1857, they might have incorporated virtually all of the present state of Nevada into their realm of colonization. But they had a continuing confrontation with the miners who built Nevada, and in the 1860s they surrendered more than half of the Great Basin to the miners coming from the west and to the jurisdiction of Carson City.[5]

As of 1940, Stegner observed, Mormon country extended approximately into the eastern third of Nevada.[6] There were the little towns on the Muddy and Virgin rivers—Overton, Bunkerville, Mesquite, Moapa, and Logandale—with about 2,000 residents in all. There were also Panaca and Alamo in Lincoln County and Preston and Lund in White Pine, outposts that had been settled by Mormons in their traditional communal manner either in the nineteenth century or early in the twentieth. Small Mormon contingents existed in Reno and Las Vegas, but they exercised little influence in state politics. Only about 10 percent of the population of the state could be considered Mormon.

In 1980, the situation was quite different. Zion was once again extending its influence southward and westward into the Great Basin and the Las Vegas Valley more rapidly than any other religious or social organization. It had not done well in the towns of the mining frontier while those communities were vigorous, but as the mid-century depression extended into the 1980s, it was mostly the gentiles—as the Mormons call their nonbelieving neighbors—who left for the greener pastures or the green-felt jungle. The best statistics available showed that nearly a fourth of all those in Nevada who professed a religious faith were Mormons, far more than those who identified themselves with any other Protestant denomination. Nearly half of all Nevada church members were Catholics, but the Mormons had 121 "wards" compared to 72 parishes for the Catholics.[7]

This meant that the Mormons were easily the fastest-growing religious group in the state, and their missionaries were the religious devotees most conspicuously active on the streets of the gambling meccas. In the eastern mining counties of Lincoln and White Pine, the religious population was more than 50 percent Latter-day Saint, and the church erected handsome new chapels in some of the economically dormant towns to signify its determination to serve the remnant in Zion. Even in Clark County there were 67 congregations, which included more than a quarter of the church-affiliated individuals in the area.[8]

This translated into far more social influence than the numbers suggest. The Mormons comprised the single most effective political contingent in the state. As we observed in the previous chapter, they were influential in the overwhelming defeat of the Equal Rights Amendment in Nevada. The First Presidency of the Church spoke eloquently and effectively against the racetrack mode of dispersing MX missiles across the Great Basin in 1982, asserting in effect that Zion's life-style should not be compromised for weapons of war. The Mormons are—and even their persistent critics are not likely to deny this assertion—a moralistic, peace-loving, responsible sort of people. They have been selected often by the Federal Bureau of Investigation (J. Edgar Hoover admired them warmly), by Howard Hughes, by the Nevada gambling control authorities, and increasingly by the Nevada voting public for service in school boards, legislative positions, judgeships, and the United States Senate. Howard Cannon, who served for four six-year terms, was the first truly successful Nevada Mormon politician. Ironically, he supported the MX proposal, and this may have contributed to his defeat in 1982.

Mormons have, in short, come into their own in Nevada, which should suggest that they would have something to say about the criminal element stalking the gambling industry and the basic ethical questions surrounding the gambling business itself.

The widespread impression is that Mormons in Nevada have adapted themselves readily to Nevada's peculiar economy and, like nearly everyone else in the state, have benefited financially from it. Wiley and Gottlieb, in their *Empires in the Sun*, described the close relation that has grown up between members of the church and the gambling establishment.[9] While the church does not condone gambling and officially discourages its members from betting and working directly at the tables as dealers, it does not discourage them from working in executive positions in the casinos, and there are prominent members of the church who have gambling licenses. Mormon bankers and real estate brokers make money from deals with some of the largest casinos, and because of church policy that encourages every faithful member to give 10 percent of his or her income to the church as "tithing," it thereby becomes a beneficiary of the gambling profits that pay the salaries of the Latter-day Saints who are employed in or near the "industry."

A more scholarly sociological study of the relationship between the peculiar Nevada social attitudes and the Mormon church was published in 1983 at Rutgers University under the title *Morals Legislation without Morality,* and it found a strange inconsistency between the attitudes of church members in Utah and their co-believers in Nevada on several issues.

> The question is how can the Nevada Mormons tolerate the existence of legalized gambling, legalized prostitution, Sunday opening of all businesses, sale of alcoholic beverages, and legal quickie marriages and divorces when they may well have both the power and the perceived moral obligation to prevent them? All of these practices seem antithetical to the sober, family centered life valued by the LDS church. If Nevada Mormons, more than most groups in the state, emphasize traditional Protestant virtues, and if morality plays any role in Nevada politics and legislation, then it should be evident in the actions of the Mormons who are an important force in the Nevada state government.[10]

The Rutgers scholars interviewed a number of Mormons, some of whom offered the same kind of rationalizations about the "industry" that Nevadans have offered for nearly a half-century. The "industry" was "clean," and there was effective regulation of it, and people who were not *directly* involved were exempt from its influence. The church was content to urge upon its members "cautious consideration" when they accepted employment that might in some way expose them to influences contrary to church teachings.[11]

Is it fair to ask whether the church itself, one of the admirable models of civic responsibility and moral family life in the contemporary West, has become in effect an accessory after the fact in the growth of an "industry" that is riddled with crime and is anathema to all the values that its revealed religion encourages? Do its bishops within Nevada and the First Presidency have any responsibility for helping to bring under control the criminal elements that have made a base on the fringe of their Zion? Might not a few of their talented members, with the backing of the church, make an important contribution to an alliance dedicated to improving the ethical level of Nevada government?

It is not unreasonable to presume that not only this church but also the Catholic clergy and the main-line Protestant denominations would lend at least strong moral support to an alliance dedicated to elementary decency in the gambling business and would support more drastic legal measures to assure it. If their denominational counterparts outside Nevada would use their moral influence to put pressure by all legal means both on the federal government and on Nevada to attack crime and the gamblers within this state who support it, even the Nevada hierarchy that is built to defend it could not be entirely deaf.

The Universities

The Nevada universities are in an ambiguous position. They, like all the other public institutions, derive much of their revenue directly or indirectly from the gambling-tourist business, and there has been a disposition of regents, presidents, and professors to tailor their policies and research whenever possible toward the economic interests of the state. When the legislature demanded to know in 1981 how all the esoteric research of the professors was benefiting Nevada, the presidents obligingly compiled a long list, which included many indications that the learned men and women of the professoriate were kissing the hands that fed them.

Yet in spite of the meager budgets that have been provided, the University of Nevada in Reno and Las Vegas maintained good research faculties dedicated not merely to the appeasement of the peculiar local institutions but also to the world of learning, and scores of these people were willing to serve the commonwealth beyond the narrow requirements of their appointments, as in the case of the review of the MX environmental impact statement. At least some of them were obviously willing to do so again to help find alternatives to the current addiction.

Among the scholars were several who were willing to look at the social and ethical implications of the "industry" itself. A national conference on gambling, initiated in Las Vegas in 1974 and repeated nearly every year thereafter into the early 1980s, explored some of the most sensitive areas of concern, including the addictive and antisocial consequences. These conferences developed a substantial body of scientific information that could be useful in providing therapy to compulsive gamblers, whether they happen to be individuals or a "sovereign" state.[12]

The Edge of the Wilderness

Beyond the churches and the academies, there are cadres of responsible and sensible people in all the trades and professions who recognize, whether they favor the "industry" or not, that it has gotten out of hand, that some of its practitioners have become too arrogant in the exercise of their privileges. For too long they have left the moral as well as the legal questions to the politicians and bureaucrats, who have proven over the decades the Jeffersonian principle that they are not good custodians of the social conscience for very long.

And out in the mining and ranching country, if one gets a little distance from the narrow swaths of interstate freeway and the airports that constitute the conduits through which the gamblers ingest their monetary narcotics, there is still a Nevada partaking of what remains of the wilderness. There is yet another generation eager to "give it a go" on the land, and their homes are reminiscent of the pioneer homesteaders' outposts, even though they are in the form of the ubiquitous mobile homes of the contemporary era. Each year they celebrate the Indian Stampede in Elko, Treasure Days in Goldfield, Pony Express Days in Ely, Heritage Days and Labor Day in Pioche, Pioneer Days in Lund, Frontier Days in Lovelock, the Basque Festivals in Elko and Winnemucca. One still finds cowboys traveling hundreds of miles to a rodeo in Eureka to compete for $700 worth of prize money in seven events, and nearly every one of the twenty little towns has or is developing a museum to celebrate its pioneer origins. Many of these Nevadans are new, but quite a few of them have approached the desert and its heritage with more respect and affection than their predecessors did. There is a Nevada out there—and in the cities as well—that has had long experience with the fast-buck artists and has not succumbed to them. With some encouragement, this Nevada might yet become an antidote to the illness that has afflicted the casino-centers.

And even if there is not actually a Sagebrush Alliance of the kind envisioned here, there is finally the redemptive power of the wilderness. The sky, the pastel mountains, and the marvelous clouds that play between them, and probably the lizards, the snakes, and even the pinions and the mountain bluebirds, have a greater staying power than we know.

NOTES

Chapter 1: The State, the Towns, and the People: 1940

1. Among the works that appeared about 1940 that are worthy of consideration are Richard G. Lillard, *Desert Challenge: An Interpretation of Nevada;* Max Miller, *Reno;* Dale L. Morgan, *The Humboldt: Highroad of the West;* Jeanne Elizabeth Wier, sponsor, *Nevada: A Guide to the Silver State;* Effie Mona Mack and Byrd Wall Sawyer, *Our State: Nevada.*

2. Russell R. Elliott, *Nevada's Twentieth-Century Mining Boom: Tonopah, Goldfield, Ely.* See also Elliott's *History of Nevada,* the best of its kind available. Another important but controversial analysis of the state's history is Gilman Ostrander, *Nevada: The Great Rotten Borough: 1859–1964.*

3. On the history of the California-Nevada boundary, see Benjamin E. Thomas, "The California-Nevada Boundary," *Annals of the Academy of American Geographers,* XLIII (March, 1952), and James W. Hulse, "The Nevada-California Boundary: The History of a Conflict," *Nevada Historical Society Quarterly,* XXIII (Summer, Fall, 1980): 87–109, 157–178.

4. Three important biographies of Nevada senators that comment on the provincialism of its political leadership are Fred L. Israel, *Nevada's Key Pittman;* Jerome E. Edwards, *Pat McCarran: Political Boss of Nevada;* and Russell R. Elliott, *Servant of Power: A Political Biography of William M. Stewart.*

5. U.S. Department of Commerce, Bureau of the Census, *Population: Number of Inhabitants,* vol. 1, p. 655; *Population: Characteristics of the Population,* pp. 719–760.

6. Wilbur S. Shepperson, *Restless Strangers: Nevada's Immigrants and Their Interpreters.*

7. Lillard, *Desert Challenge,* p. 4.

8. Ibid., p. 307.

9. Ibid., pp. 46–47.

Chapter 2: The Four Nevadas Revisited: 1980

1. Oscar Lewis, *Sagebrush Casinos: The Story of Legal Gambling in Nevada,* p. 113.

2. Walter Van Tilburg Clark, "Reno: The City State," in Ray B. West, Jr., ed., *Rocky Mountain Cities,* pp. 30–31. Clark's novel *The City of Trembling Leaves* contains some elegant

prose and is of permanent value as description of the landscape around Reno. Also of interest is a collection of essays on him, Charlton G. Laird, ed., *Walter Van Tilburg Clark: Critiques.*

3. In 1950, Senator Pat McCarran, Senator George W. Malone, and Congressman Walter Baring all had their main Nevada offices within a few doors of the courthouse and city hall in Reno.

4. Dale L. Morgan, *The Humboldt: Highroad of the West,* pp. 340–341.

5. U.S. Department of Commerce, Bureau of the Census, *Population: Number of Inhabitants,* vol. 1, p. 655; U.S. Department of Commerce, Bureau of the Census, *1980 Census of Population,* vol. 1, chapter A, "Number of Inhabitants: Nevada" (October, 1981), 30–10 Nevada.

6. Ibid. Again I have found it more meaningful to use township rather than municipal figures.

7. Robert Laxalt, "The Other Nevada," *National Geographic,* 145, No. 6 (June, 1974): 733–761.

8. Those who take comfort in the nostalgia evoked by old railroads have been well served by David F. Myrick, *Railroads of Nevada and Eastern California;* by Gilbert H. Kneiss, *Bonanza Railroads;* and by Lucius Beebe and Charles Clegg, *Steamcars to the Comstock.* They can take even more substantial gratification from the fine work of the Nevada State Museum in Carson City, which since 1980 has done much to restore the surviving rolling stock of the Virginia & Truckee.

9. Edna B. Patterson, Louise A. Ulph, and Victor Goodwin, *Nevada's Northeastern Frontier,* p. 670.

10. Wier, sponsor, *Nevada,* p. 183.

11. *Las Vegas Age* (March 9, 1940), 2: 1.

12. Two descriptions of the growth of Las Vegas by local residents with a journalistic flair are Stanley W. Paher, *Las Vegas: As It Began—As It Grew,* and Ralph Pearl, *Las Vegas Is My Beat.*

13. The most satisfactory comprehensive study of the period before 1960 is Perry Bruce Kaufman, "The Best City of Them All: A History of Las Vegas, 1930–1960." On the city's reputation, see pp. 105–166.

14. Ibid., pp. 421–426.

15. Ibid., pp. 159–161.

16. "Las Vegas Plans Its Future," General Master Plan for the City of Las Vegas, Nevada.

17. Ibid., pp. 19–20.

18. Ibid., p. 15.

19. David T. Friendly, "Snake Eyes for Las Vegas," *Newsweek* (August 23, 1982): 54.

20. Tim Carlson and Ann Cooper, eds., *Las Vegas Perspectives—1981.*

21. Ibid., pp. 42–45.

22. Franklin J. Bills et al., *City of North Las Vegas, Nevada: 1973,* Community Analysis and Evaluation Program, pp. 51–53.

23. Ibid., p. 53.

24. These are summarized in Elbert B. Edwards, *200 Years in Nevada,* pp. 351–353.

25. City of Henderson and Henderson Chamber of Commerce, *It's Happening in Henderson,* p. 6.

Chapter 3: The Struggles for Water

1. For a comprehensive summary of the water situation in the Great Basin, see Samuel G. Houghton, *A Trace of Desert Waters: The Great Basin Story.* An excellent discussion of the situation on the Colorado River is Philip L. Fradkin, *A River No More: The Colorado River and the West.*

2. Nevada Bureau of Mines and U.S. Geological Survey, *Mineral and Water Resources of Nevada,* Bulletin 65, p. 273.

3. *Winters* v. *United States,* 207 U.S. 564 (1908).

4. *United States* v. *Orr Water Ditch Co.,* Equity No. 3-A, U.S. District Court for Nevada (1944).

5. Lillard, *Desert Challenge*, pp. 61–73.

6. *United States and Pyramid Lake Paiute Tribe* v. *Truckee-Carson Irrigation District, et al.*, Civil No. R-1987-JBA. December 12, 1977.

7. John M. Townley, *Turn This Water into Gold: The Story of the Newlands Project*, p. 133.

8. The Ninth Circuit Court ruling is 649 F. 2d 1286 (9th Circuit 1981). The U.S. Supreme Court ruling is *Nevada* v. *United States*, No. 81-2245, decided June 24, 1983.

9. Douglas H. Strong, *Tahoe: An Environmental History*, p. xiii.

10. Ibid., pp. 50–51.

11. Ibid., pp. 186–187.

12. Ibid., pp. 108–110. See also the informative article by Donald J. Pisani, "The Strange Death of the California-Nevada Compact: A Study in Interstate Water Negotiations," *Pacific Historical Review*, 47 (November, 1978): 637–658.

13. Strong, *Tahoe*, pp. 52–53.

14. *Statutes of Nevada . . . 1939*, chapter 178, pp. 274–279.

15. The most informative study is Florence Lee Jones and John F. Cahlan, *Water: A History of Las Vegas*. Jones and Cahlan collaborated on the first volume, which chronicles the main events before 1955, and Jones wrote the second volume.

16. Ibid., vol. II, p. 1.

17. Nevada Bureau of Mines and U.S. Geological Survey, *Mineral and Water Resources*, p. 310.

18. *Arizona* v. *California*, 323 U.S. 546 (1963). For a discussion of the history of this case, see Jones, *Water*, vol. II, pp. 49–50, 63–64. The Supreme Court added to its findings in *Arizona* v. *California*, No. 8, orig. decided March 30, 1983.

19. Montgomery Engineers of Nevada, *Water for Nevada*, Special Planning Report (January, 1971).

20. Fradkin, *A River No More*, pp. 16–17.

21. A. Berry Crawford and Dean F. Peterson, eds., *Environmental Management in the Colorado River Basin*.

22. The foremost study of this subject is by John W. Hess and Martin D. Mifflin, *A Feasibility Study of Water Production from Deep Carbonate Aquifers in Nevada*.

23. Nevada Bureau of Mines and U.S. Geological Survey, *Mineral and Water Resources*, pp. 299–300.

24. *Nevada State Journal* (October 21, 1982), 2C: 2–4.

25. Desert Research Institute, *Quarterly Newsletter*, I, No. 2 (March, 1973); "Final Report on the Pyramid Lake Pilot Project, 1970–1975," mimeographed report prepared by the Laboratory of Atmospheric Physics, Desert Research Institute (January, 1977).

26. Desert Research Institute, Atmospheric Sciences Center, "1978–1980 State Weather Modification Program: Biennial Report," pp. 1–5; DRI, "President's Annual Report," 1977–1978, pp. 14–15.

27. *Cappaert et al.* v. *United States*, 426 U.S. 128 (1975).

28. Division of Water Planning, State of Nevada, "Water Conservation in Nevada," Water Planning Report No. 1, mimeographed.

29. Legislative Commission of the Legislative Counsel Bureau, "Water Problems in the State," Bulletin No. 81–5 (October, 1980), p. vi.

Chapter 4: The Land and Its Uses

1. John McPhee, *Basin and Range*, p. 45.

2. Public Land Law Review Commission, *One Third of the Nation's Land*, A Report to the President and the Congress by the Public Land Law Review Commission.

3. Ibid., p. 1.

4. Ibid., pp. 2–7.

5. Public Law 94-579, 94th Congress, enacted October 21, 1976.

6. *Statutes of Nevada . . . 1979,* chapter 633, pp. 1362–1367.

7. *Constitution of the State of Nevada, 1864* (Ordinance).

8. *Newsweek,* 94 (September 17, 1979): 31–40.

9. Ibid., p. 39.

10. Peter Stoler et al., "Land Sale of the Century," *Time,* 120 (August 23, 1982): 16–22.

11. Fradkin, *A River No More,* pp. 83–84.

12. U.S. Department of the Interior, Bureau of Land Management, "The Nation's Public Lands: A Briefing Package" (November 1, 1981), pp. 3–4.

13. Ibid., pp. 17ff.

14. U.S. Department of Agriculture, Forest Service, "An Assessment of the Forest and Range Land Situation in the United States" (January, 1980).

15. Robert F. Burford, "Rangeland Policies for the Future," *Your Public Lands,* 32 (Spring, 1982): 5.

16. U.S. Air Force, "Brief Facts about MX" (1980).

17. Stansfield Turner, "Why We Shouldn't Build the MX," *New York Times Magazine* (March 29, 1981): 14–17, 44–46.

18. Donald M. Snow, "MX: Maginot Line of the 1980s," *Bulletin of the Atomic Scientists,* 36 (November, 1980): 21–25.

19. "The True Cost of MX," *Nucleus, A Report to the Union of Concerned Scientists Sponsors,* 3 (Fall–Winter, 1980): 2.

20. U.S. Department of the Air Force *Environmental Impact Analysis Process: Deployment Area Selection and Land Withdrawal/Acquisition Draft Environmental Impact Statement* (DEIS) December, 1980.

21. State of Nevada, "Official Response to the United States Air Force Deployment Area Selection and Land Withdrawal/Acquisition Draft Environmental Impact Statement" (April 30, 1981).

22. *Nevada State Journal* (August 9, 1980): 12.

23. *New York Times,* Y (September 14, 1982), 9: 1–5.

24. Thomas P. O'Farrell and LaVerne A. Emery, *Ecology of the Nevada Test Site: A Narrative Summary and Annotated Bibliography.*

Chapter 5: The Utopia for Gamblers

1. Mark Twain, *Roughing It,* p. 250.

2. Walter Van Tilburg Clark, "Nevada's Fateful Desert," *Holiday,* 22 (November, 1957): 76–77, 100–103.

3. Ibid., p. 100.

4. Wier, sponsor, *Nevada,* p. 4.

5. Ibid.

6. The involvement of criminal elements in Nevada gambling has been exhaustively discussed in the press and in scores of books. Among the best of these are Elliott, *History of Nevada;* Wallace Turner, *Gamblers' Money: A New Force in American Life;* and Robert Laxalt, *Nevada: A Bicentennial History.* There are also good historical summaries of the legal and economic experiences of the business in William R. Eadington and James S. Hattori, "Gambling in Nevada: Legislative History and Economic Trends," a mimeographed report by the Bureau of Business and Economic Research, Paper No. 77-17 and in William R. Eadington, "The Evolution of Corporate Gambling in Nevada," *Nevada Review of Business and Economics,* VI, No. 1 (Spring, 1982): 13–22.

7. U.S. Senate, *Third Interim Report of the Special Committee to Investigate Crime in Interstate Commerce*, Report No. 307, 82d Congress, p. 2.

8. Ibid., pp. 90–94.

9. McCarran's position is contained in a 1951 letter, which is quoted at length in Edwards, *Pat McCarran*, p. 153f.

10. This case has been widely discussed in recent Nevada histories. See especially Elliott, *History of Nevada*, pp. 329–333; and Mary Ellen Glass, *Nevada's Turbulent '50s: Decade of Political and Economic Change*, pp. 25–38.

11. *Journal of the Assembly*, 48th Session, Nevada Legislature . . . 1957, pp. 361–362.

12. *Nevada Tax Commission* v. *Hicks et al.*, Nevada Reports (1957), p. 119.

13. Nevada Gaming Commission, *Legalized Gambling in Nevada: Its History, Economics, and Control*, prepared under the direction of Walter C. Wilson, executive secretary of the Nevada Gaming Commission, p. 13.

14. Turner, *Gamblers' Money*.

15. Ibid., p. 2.

16. *New York Times* (September 2, 1966), 1: 1, 32: 1.

17. *Washington Post* (August 7, 1966): A-4.

18. The articles appeared in the *Las Vegas Sun* and in the Reno newspapers in February and March of 1967. They were written by Gabriel R. Vogliotti, executive director of the association.

19. Donald L. Barlett and James B. Steele, *Empire: The Life, Legend, and Madness of Howard Hughes*, pp. 296ff.

20. James W. Hulse, *The University of Nevada: A Centennial History*, p. 236.

21. Barlett and Steele, *Empire*, pp. 440–441.

22. Ibid., pp. 488–489.

23. Peter Wiley and Robert Gottlieb, *Empires in the Sun: The Rise of the New American West*, p. 203.

24. Robert Laxalt, *Nevada: A Bicentennial History*, p. 105.

25. Hannifan as quoted in Laxalt, *Nevada*, p. 112.

26. Laxalt, *Nevada*, p. 110.

27. *Nevada State Journal* (November 18, 1978), 1: 1–6, 26: 1–3.

28. *Wall Street Journal* (August 10, 1979), 1: 1, 21: 1–3.

29. *Nevada State Journal* (August 27, 1979), 1: 1–6, 14: 1–6.

30. *Nevada State Journal* (January 10, 1980), 20: 1–6.

31. *Nevada State Journal* (March 17, 1981), 11: 1–3.

32. Jerome H. Skolnick, *House of Cards: The Legalization and Control of Casino Gambling*.

33. Ibid., pp. 335–344.

34. Ibid., pp. 344–345.

35. Ibid., p. 356. For another discussion of Nevada's efforts to control the criminal element, see the forthcoming second edition of Elliott's *History of Nevada*.

36. For a typical example of the national coverage, see *Time*, 117 (February 23, 1981): 23.

37. Tom Wolfe, *The Kandy-Kolored Tangerine-Flake Streamline Baby*, p. xvi.

38. Ibid., pp. 3–28.

Chapter 6: Beyond the Glitter: A State Without a Conscience

1. Albert Deutsch, "The Sorry State of Nevada," *Collier's*, 135 (March 18, 1955): 74–85.

2. Ibid., p. 85.

3. Elmer R. Rusco, "Welfare in Nevada: The Great Anomaly," *Nevada Public Affairs Review: Social Problems—Nevada's Solutions*, No. 1 (1980): 8–18.

4. Ibid., p. 12.

5. Ibid., p. 16.

6. Richard Siegel and Ellen Pillard, "Information, Innovation, and Social Policy," *Nevada Public Affairs Review: Social Problems—Nevada's Solutions,* No. 1 (1980): 3. Siegel and Pillard drew their data from the *Statistical Abstracts of the United States* for 1978, published by the U.S. Department of Commerce.

7. Charles R. Zeh, "Nevada's Response to Crime: Rethinking the Use of Incarceration," in *Nevada Public Affairs Review: Social Problems—Nevada's Solutions,* No. 1 (1980): 37.

8. An informative essay on early civil rights legislation in Nevada is Joseph N. Crowley, "Race and Residence: The Politics of Open Housing in Nevada," in Eleanore Bushnell, ed., *Sagebrush and Neon: Studies in Nevada Politics,* pp. 59–79.

9. *Statutes of Nevada . . . 1961,* chapter 364, pp. 731–733. For later versions, see *Nevada Revised Statutes,* 233.010 to 233.080.

10. Elmer R. Rusco, *Minority Groups in Nevada,* p. 2ff.

11. *Nevada Commission on Equal Rights of Citizens* v. *Lindsay Smith,* Nevada Reports, 80, (1964), pp. 469–476.

12. Crowley, "Race and Residence," pp. 74–75.

13. Elmer R. Rusco, "Racial Discrimination in Employment in Nevada: A Continuing Problem," *Governmental Research Newsletter,* University of Nevada Bureau of Governmental Research, XI, No. 5 (February, 1973).

14. Jack D. Forbes, *Nevada Indians Speak,* pp. 13–14.

15. Ibid., pp. 189–194.

16. Robert S. Pelcyger, "The Winters Doctrine and the Greening of the Reservations," *Journal of Contemporary Law,* 4 (Winter, 1977): 34, 36.

17. See discussion of the Truckee River case in chapter 3, above.

18. Joe Alley, *The Las Vegas Paiutes: A Short History.*

19. Nellie Shaw Harnar, *Indians of the Coo-yu-ee Pah (Pyramid Lake): The History of the Pyramid Lake Indians.*

20. Edward C. Johnson, *Walker River Paiutes: A Tribal History.*

21. For an informed treatment of the Hispanics in the region, see A. J. Jaffe et al., *The Changing Demography of Spanish Americans.*

22. U.S. Department of Commerce, Bureau of the Census, *1980 Census of Population,* "Nevada," 30–10.

23. Shepperson, *Restless Strangers,* pp. 116–121.

24. Andrew Hacker, "E.R.A.—R.I.P.," *Harper's,* 261 (September, 1980).

25. Superintendent of Public Instruction, *Biennial Report . . . July 1, 1940, to June 30, 1942,* pp. 60–63.

26. George Peabody College for Teachers, *Public Education in Nevada,* pp. 273–277. For a good summary of the political activities leading to the reform of the 1950s, see Glass, *Nevada's Turbulent '50s,* pp. 49–60.

27. Glen W. Atkinson and Thomas A. Sears, "Research Report: School Finance and Tax Reform in Nevada," p. 44.

28. Governor Mike O'Callaghan, "Message to the Legislature of Nevada, Fifty-Sixth Session, 1971," *Journal of the Assembly . . . 1971,* p. 27.

29. Governor Mike O'Callaghan, "Message of the Governor to the Legislature of Nevada: Fifty-Ninth Session, 1977," *Journal of the Assembly . . . 1977,* p. 33.

30. W. Vance Grant and Leo J. Eiden, *Digest of Education Statistics 1981,* National Center for Education Statistics, U.S. Department of Education, p. 26.

31. Ibid., p. 88.

32. *Nevada State Journal* (June 3, 1981), 13: 1–2.

33. Frederick Rudolph, *The American College and University: A History.*

34. *Bulletin of the University of Nevada: Catalog Issue, 1941–1942,* XXXV, No. 3 (June 15, 1941); "Report of the Regents of the University of Nevada . . ., July 1, 1940–June 30, 1942," *University of Nevada Bulletin,* XXXVI, No. 5 (August 15, 1942).

35. Hulse, *The University of Nevada*, pp. 52–59. For a detailed description of the Stout era and its problems, see Dean E. McHenry et al., *The University of Nevada: An Appraisal*, Legislative Counsel Bureau Report No. 28.

36. Governor Robert List, "Message to the Legislature of Nevada, Sixtieth Session, 1979, *Journal of the Assembly . . . 1979*, p. 55.

Chapter 7: A Fifth Nevada: With a Conscience?

1. As late as December, 1984, the Las Vegas Metropolitan Police issued a report saying that at least eighteen organized crime "families" were operating within the city (*Reno Gazette-Journal* [December 16, 1984], 1A: 2–5).

2. "Gambling," *The New Catholic Encyclopedia* (New York: McGraw Hill, 1967), vol. VI, p. 276.

3. Ibid.

4. Wallace Stegner, *Mormon Country*.

5. Elliott, *History of Nevada*, pp. 49–57; James W. Hulse, *The Nevada Adventure: A History*, pp. 65–82.

6. Stegner, *Mormon Country*, p. 35.

7. Bernard Quinn et al., *Churches and Church Membership in the United States 1980*, pp. 19–20.

8. Ibid., pp. 184–185.

9. Wiley and Gottlieb, *Empires in the Sun*, pp. 198–201.

10. John F. Galliher and John R. Cross, *Morals Legislation without Morality: The Case of Nevada*, pp. 76–77.

11. Ibid., pp. 77–79.

12. The work of the first conference was published in William R. Eadington, ed., *Gambling and Society: Interdisciplinary Studies on the Subject of Gambling*. For a sample of more recent studies, see William R. Eadington, ed., *Pathological Gambling: Theory and Practice*, vol. I, and *Legal, Economic, and Humanistic Perspectives on Gambling*, vol. IX, *The Gambling Papers: Proceedings of the Fifth National Conference on Gambling and Risk Taking*.

BIBLIOGRAPHY

Alley, Joe. *The Las Vegas Paiutes: A Short History* (Las Vegas: Las Vegas Tribe of Paiutes, 1977).

Atkinson, Glen W., and Thomas A. Sears. "Research Report: School Finance and Tax Reform in Nevada," typescript distributed by the College of Business Administration, University of Nevada, 1979.

Barlett, Donald L., and James B. Steele. *Empire: The Life, Legend, and Madness of Howard Hughes* (New York: W. W. Norton, 1979).

Beebe, Lucius, and Charles Clegg. *Steamcars to the Comstock* (Berkeley: Howell-North, 1957).

Bills, Franklin J., et al. *City of North Las Vegas, Nevada: 1973*, Community Analysis and Evaluation Program (North Las Vegas: City of North Las Vegas, 1973).

Burford, Robert F. "Rangeland Policies for the Future," *Your Public Lands*, 32 (Spring, 1982).

Bushnell, Eleanore, and Don W. Driggs. *The Nevada Constitution: Origin and Growth*, 6th ed. (Reno: University of Nevada Press, 1984).

Carlson, Helen S. *Nevada Place Names: A Geographical Dictionary* (Reno: University of Nevada Press, 1974).

Carlson, Tim, and Ann Cooper, eds. *Las Vegas Perspectives—1981* (Las Vegas: Las Vegas Review-Journal* et al., 1981).

Clark, Walter Van Tilburg. "Nevada's Fateful Desert," *Holiday*, 22 (November, 1957): 76–77, 100–103.

———. "Reno: The City State," in Ray. B. West, Jr., ed., *Rocky Mountain Cities* (New York: W. W. Norton, 1949), pp. 30–31.

Crawford, A. Berry, and Dean F. Peterson, eds. *Environmental Management in the Colorado River Basin* (Logan: Utah State University Press, 1974).

Crowley, Joseph N. "Race and Residence: The Politics of Open Housing in Nevada," in Eleanore Bushnell, ed., *Sagebrush and Neon: Studies in Nevada Politics*, rev. ed. (Reno: University of Nevada Bureau of Government Research, 1976).

Deutsch, Albert. "The Sorry State of Nevada," *Collier's*, 135 (March 18, 1955), pp. 74–85.

Eadington, William R. "The Evolution of Corporate Gambling in Nevada," *Nevada Review of Business and Economics*, VI, No. 1 (Spring, 1982): 13–22.

———, ed. *Gambling and Society: Interdisciplinary Studies on the Subject of Gambling* (Springfield, Ill.: Charles C. Thomas, 1976).

131

————, ed. *The Gambling Papers: Proceedings of the Fifth National Conference on Gambling and Risk Taking* (Reno: University of Nevada Bureau of Business and Economic Research, 1982), vols. I and IX.

Eadington, William R., and James S. Hattori. "Gambling in Nevada: Legislative History and Economic Trends," a mimeographed report by the Bureau of Business and Economic Research, Paper No. 77–17, University of Nevada, 1977.

Edwards, Elbert B. *200 Years in Nevada* (Salt Lake City: Publishers Press, 1978).

Edwards, Jerome E. *Pat McCarran: Political Boss of Nevada* (Reno: University of Nevada Press, 1982).

Elliott, Russell R. *History of Nevada* (Lincoln: University of Nebraska Press, 1973).

————. *Nevada's Twentieth-Century Mining Boom: Tonopah, Goldfield, Ely* (Reno: University of Nevada Press, 1966).

————. *Servant of Power: A Political Biography of William M. Stewart* (Reno: University of Nevada Press, 1983).

Elliott, Russell R., and Helen J. Poulton. *Writings on Nevada: A Selected Bibliography* (Reno: University of Nevada Press, 1963).

Forbes, Jack D. *Nevada Indians Speak* (Reno: University of Nevada Press, 1967).

Fradkin, Philip L. *A River No More: The Colorado River and the West* (New York: Alfred A. Knopf, 1981).

Friendly, David T. "Snake Eyes for Las Vegas," *Newsweek* (August 23, 1982): 54.

Galliher, John F., and John R. Cross. *Morals Legislation without Morality: The Case of Nevada* (New Brunswick, N.J.: Rutgers University Press, 1983).

George Peabody College for Teachers. *Public Education in Nevada* (Nashville: Peabody, 1954).

Glass, Mary Ellen. *Nevada's Turbulent '50s: Decade of Political and Economic Change* (Reno: University of Nevada Press, 1981).

Grant, W. Vance, and Leo J. Eiden. *Digest of Education Statistics 1981,* National Center for Education Statistics, U.S. Department of Education (Washington, D.C.: U.S. Government Printing Office, 1981).

Hacker, Andrew. "E.R.A.—R.I.P." *Harper's,* 261 (September, 1980): 10–14.

Harnar, Nellie Shaw. *Indians of the Coo-yu-ee Pah (Pyramid Lake): The History of the Pyramid Lake Indians* (Sparks, Nev.: Dave's Printing and Publishing, 1974).

Hart, John. *Hiking the Great Basin: The High Country of California, Oregon, Nevada, and Utah* (San Francisco: Sierra Club Books, 1981).

Henderson, City of, and Henderson Chamber of Commerce. *It's Happening in Henderson* (Henderson: Sage Printing, October, 1981).

Hess, John W., and Martin D. Mifflin. *A Feasibility Study of Water Production from Deep Carbonate Aquifers in Nevada* (Las Vegas: Desert Research Institute, University of Nevada System, September, 1978).

Houghton, Samuel G. *A Trace of Desert Waters: The Great Basin Story* (Glendale, Cal.: Arthur H. Clark Co., 1976).

Hulse, James W. *The Nevada Adventure: A History* (Reno: University of Nevada Press, 1965; 5th ed., 1981).

————. "The Nevada-California Boundary: The History of a Conflict," *Nevada Historical Society Quarterly,* XXIII (Summer, Fall, 1980): 87–109, 157–178.

————. *The University of Nevada: A Centennial History* (Reno: University of Nevada Press, 1974).

Hundley, Norris. *Water and the West: The Colorado River Compact and the Politics of Water in the American West* (Berkeley: University of California Press, 1975).

Israel, Fred L. *Nevada's Key Pittman* (Lincoln: University of Nebraska Press, 1963).

Jaffe, A. J. et al. *The Changing Demography of Spanish Americans* (New York: Academic Press, 1980).

Johnson, Edward C. *Walker River Paiutes: A Tribal History* (Schurz, Nev.: Walker River Paiute Tribe, 1975).

Jones, Florence Lee, and John F. Cahlan. *Water: A History of Las Vegas*, 2 vols. (Las Vegas: Las Vegas Valley Water District, 1975).

Kaufman, Perry Bruce. "The Best City of Them All: A History of Las Vegas, 1930–1960." Ph.D. dissertation, University of California–Santa Barbara, 1974.

Kneiss, Gilbert H. *Bonanza Railroads* (Stanford: Stanford University Press, 1941).

Laird, Charlton G., ed. *Walter Van Tilburg Clark: Critiques* (Reno: University of Nevada Press, 1983).

Lamm, Richard D., and Michael McCarthy. *The Angry West: A Vulnerable Land and Its Future* (Boston: Houghton Mifflin, 1982).

Las Vegas Age (March 9, 1940).

"Las Vegas Plans Its Future," General Master Plan for the City of Las Vegas, Nevada (1959).

Laxalt, Robert. *Nevada: A Bicentennial History* (New York: W. W. Norton, 1977).

———. "The Other Nevada," *National Geographic,* 145, No. 6 (June, 1974): 733–761.

Lewis, Oscar. *Sagebrush Casinos: The Story of Legal Gambling in Nevada* (Garden City, N.Y.: Doubleday, 1953).

Lillard, Richard G. *Desert Challenge: An Interpretation of Nevada* (New York: Alfred A. Knopf, 1942; reprinted by Knopf in 1949 and by the University of Nebraska in 1966).

McHenry, Dean E., et al. *The University of Nevada: An Appraisal,* Legislative Counsel Bureau Report No. 28 (Carson City: State Printing Office, 1956).

McPhee, John. *Basin and Range* (New York: Farrar, Straus, Giroux, 1980).

Mack, Effie Mona, and Byrd Wall Sawyer. *Our State: Nevada* (Caldwell, Ida.: Caxton Printers, 1940).

Miller, Max. *Reno* (New York: Dodd, Mead, 1941).

Montgomery Engineers of Nevada. *Water for Nevada,* Special Planning Report (January, 1971).

Morgan, Dale L. *The Humboldt: Highroad of the West* (New York: Farrar and Rinehart, 1943).

Myrick, David F. *Railroads of Nevada and Eastern California.* vol. 1, *The Northern Roads;* vol. 2, *The Southern Roads* (Berkeley: Howell-North, 1962, 1963).

Nevada. Assembly. *Journal of the Assembly,* 48th Session, Nevada Legislature . . . 1957 (Carson City: State Printing Office, 1957).

———. Bureau of Mines and U.S. Geological Survey. *Mineral and Water Resources in Nevada* (Reno: University of Nevada, Mackay School of Mines, 1964), Bulletin 65, p. 273.

———. *Constitution of the State of Nevada.* Ordinance.

———. Division of Water Planning. "Water Conservation in Nevada," mimeographed, Report No. 1 (Carson City, 1979).

———. Gaming Commission. *Legalized Gambling in Nevada: Its History, Economics, and Control,* prepared under the direction of Walter C. Wilson, executive secretary of the Nevada Gaming Commission (Carson City: State Printing Office, 1962).

———. Governor. "Message to the Legislature of Nevada, Fifty-Sixth Session, 1971," by Mike O'Callaghan. *Journal of the Assembly . . . 1971* (Carson City: State Printing Office, 1972).

———. "Message to the Legislature of Nevada, Fifty-Ninth Session, 1977," by Mike O'Callaghan, *Journal of the Assembly . . . 1977* (Carson City: State Printing Office, 1978).

———. "Message to the Legislature of Nevada, Sixtieth Session, 1979," *Journal of the Assembly . . . 1979* (Carson City: State Printing Office, 1980).

———. Legislative Commission of the Legislative Counsel Bureau. "Water Problems in the State," Bulletin No. 81–5 (October, 1980).

———. "Official Response to the United States Air Force Deployment Area Selection and Land Withdrawal/Acquisition Draft Environmental Impact Statement" (Carson City, April 30, 1981).

———. *Statutes of Nevada . . . 1939,* chapter 178, pp. 274–279.

———. *Statutes of Nevada . . . 1961,* chapter 364, pp. 731–733.

———. *Statutes of Nevada . . . 1979,* chapter 633, pp. 1362–1367.

———. Superintendent of Public Instruction. *Biennial Report . . . July 1, 1940 to June 30, 1942* (Carson City: State Printing Office, 1943).

――――. Supreme Court. *Nevada Commission on Equal Rights of Citizens* v. *Lindsay Smith*, Nevada Reports, 80 (1964), pp. 469–476.

――――. *Nevada Tax Commission* v. *Hicks, et al.*, 73, Nevada Reports, (1957), pp. 115–135.

Nevada State Journal (November 18, 1978), 1: 1–6; 26: 1–3; (August 27, 1979), 1: 1–6, 14: 1–6; (January 10, 1980), 20: 1–6; (August 9, 1980), p. 12; (March 17, 1981), 11: 1–3; (June 3, 1981), 13: 1–2; (October 21, 1982), 2C: 2–4.

Newsweek, 94 (September 17, 1979): 31–40.

New York Times (September 2, 1966) 1: 1, 32: 1; Y (September 14, 1982), 9: 1–5.

O'Farrell, Thomas P., and LaVerne A. Emery, *Ecology of the Nevada Test Site: A Narrative Summary and Annotated Bibliography* (Springfield, Va.: U.S. Department of Commerce, National Technical Information Services, May, 1976).

Ostrander, Gilman. *Nevada: The Great Rotten Borough: 1859–1964* (New York: Alfred A. Knopf, 1966).

Paher, Stanley W. *Las Vegas: As It Began—As It Grew*, with maps and illustrations by Roy E. Purcell (Las Vegas: Nevada Publications, 1971).

――――. *Nevada Ghost Towns and Mining Camps* (Berkeley: Howell-North, 1970).

Patterson, Edna B., Louise A. Ulph, and Victor Goodwin. *Nevada's Northeastern Frontier* (Sparks, Nev.: Western Printing and Publishing, 1969).

Pearl, Ralph. *Las Vegas Is My Beat* (Secaucus, N.J.: Lyle Stuart, 1973).

Pelcyger, Robert S. "The Winters Doctrine and the Greening of the Reservations," *Journal of Contemporary Law*, 4 (Winter, 1977): 19–37.

Pisani, Donald J. "Federal Reclamation and Water Rights in Nevada," *Agricultural History*, 51 (July, 1977): 540–558.

――――. "The Strange Death of the California-Nevada Compact: A Study in Interstate Water Negotiations," *Pacific Historical Review*, 47 (November, 1978): 637–658.

Pomeroy, Earl. *The Pacific Slope: A History of California, Oregon, Washington, Idaho, Utah, and Nevada* (New York: Alfred A. Knopf, 1965).

Quinn, Bernard, et al. *Churches and Church Membership in the United States 1980* (Atlanta: Glenmary Research Center, 1982).

Ronald, Ann. *The New West of Edward Abbey* (Albuquerque: University of New Mexico Press, 1982).

Rowley, William D. *Reno: Hub of the Washoe Country* (Woodland Hills, Calif.: Windsor Publications, 1984).

Rudolph, Frederick. *The American College and University: A History* (New York: Alfred A. Knopf, 1962).

Rusco, Elmer R. *Minority Groups in Nevada* (Reno: University of Nevada Bureau of Governmental Research, 1966).

――――. "The Organization of the Te-Moak Bands of Western Shoshone," *Nevada Historical Society Quarterly*, XXV (Fall, 1972): 175–196.

――――. "Racial Discrimination in Employment in Nevada: A Continuing Problem," *Governmental Research Newsletter*, University of Nevada Bureau of Governmental Research, XI, No. 5 (February, 1973).

――――. "Welfare in Nevada: The Great Anomaly," *Nevada Public Affairs Review: Social Problems—Nevada's Solutions*, No. 1 (Reno: University of Nevada Bureau of Governmental Research, 1980), pp. 8–18.

Shepperson, Wilbur S. *Restless Strangers: Nevada's Immigrants and Their Interpreters* (Reno: University of Nevada Press, 1970).

Siegel, Richard, and Ellen Pillard, "Information, Innovation, and Social Policy," *Nevada Public Affairs Review: Social Problems—Nevada's Solutions*, No. 1 (Reno: University of Nevada Bureau of Governmental Research, 1980), pp. 3–7.

Skolnick, Jerome H. *House of Cards: The Legalization and Control of Casino Gambling* (Boston: Little, Brown, 1978).

Smith, Harold T. "New Deal Relief Programs in Nevada: 1933–1935," Ph.D. dissertation, University of Nevada–Reno, 1972.

Snow, Donald M. "MX: Maginot Line of the 1980s," *Bulletin of the Atomic Scientists,* 36 (November, 1980): 21–25.

Stegner, Wallace. *Mormon Country* (Lincoln: University of Nebraska Press, 1981; reprint of the 1942 edition).

Stoler, Peter, et al. "Land Sale of the Century," *Time,* 120 (August 23, 1982): 16–22.

Strong, Douglas H. *Tahoe: An Environmental History* (Lincoln: University of Nebraska Press, 1984).

Thomas, Benjamin E. "The California-Nevada Boundary," *Annals of the Academy of American Geographers,* XLIII (March, 1952):

Townley, John M. *Tough Little Town on the Truckee: Reno—1868–1900* (Reno: Great Basin Studies Center, 1983).

———. *Turn This Water into Gold: The Story of the Newlands Project* (Reno: Nevada Historical Society, 1977).

"The True Cost of MX," *Nucleus, A Report to the Union of Concerned Scientist Sponsors,* 3 (Fall–Winter, 1980).

Turner, Stansfield. "Why We Shouldn't Build the MX," *New York Times Magazine* (March 29, 1981): 14–17, 44–46.

Turner, Wallace. *Gamblers' Money: A New Force in American Life* (Boston: Houghton Mifflin, 1965).

Twain, Mark. *Roughing It,* introduction by Rodman W. Paul (New York: Holt, Rinehart and Winston, 1953).

United States. Department of the Air Force. *Environmental Impact Analysis Process: Deployment Area Selection and Land Withdrawal/Acquisition Draft Environmental Impact Statement* (DEIS) (December, 1980).

———. Systems Command. MX Public Service Communications. "Brief Facts about MX," Andrews Air Force Base, Maryland, 1980.

———. Department of Agriculture. Forest Service. "An Assessment of the Forest and Range Land Situation in the United States" (January, 1980).

———. Department of Commerce. Bureau of the Census. *Population: Number of Inhabitants* (Washington, D.C.: U.S. Government Printing Office, 1942), vol. 1, p. 655.

———. *Population: Characteristics of the Population* (Washington, D.C.: U.S. Government Printing Office, 1943), pp. 719–760.

———. *1980 Census of Population,* vol. 1, chapter A, "Number of Inhabitants: Nevada" (October, 1981), 30–10 Nevada.

———. Department of the Interior. Bureau of Land Management. "The Nation's Public Lands: A Briefing Package" (November 1, 1981).

———. District Court for Nevada. *United States v. Orr Water Ditch Company,* Equity No. 3–A (1944).

———. *United States and Pyramid Lake Paiute Tribe v. Truckee-Carson Irrigation District, et al.,* Civil No. R-1987-JBA, December 12, 1977.

———. Public Land Law Review Commission. *One Third of the Nation's Land* (Washington, D.C.: Government Printing Office, June, 1970).

———. Senate. *Third Interim Report of the Special Committee to Investigate Crime in Interstate Commerce,* Report No. 307, 82d Congress (Washington, D.C.: U.S. Government Printing Office, 1951).

———. *Statutes at Large.* Public Law 94–579, 94th Congress, enacted October 21, 1976.

———. Supreme Court. *Arizona v. California.* 323 U.S. 546 (1963), supplemented by No. 8, orig. decided March 30, 1983.

———. *Cappaert et al. v. United States,* 426 U.S. 128 (1975).

———. *Nevada v. United States,* No. 81–2245, decided June 24, 1983.

————. *Winters* v. *United States,* 207 U.S. 564 (1908).

University of Nevada. *Bulletin of the University of Nevada: Catalog Issue, 1941–1942,* XXXV, No. 3 (June 15, 1941).

————. "Report of the Regents of the University of Nevada . . . , July 1, 1940–June 30, 1942," *University of Nevada Bulletin,* XXXVI, No. 5 (August 15, 1942).

————. Desert Research Institute. *Quarterly Newsletter,* I, No. 2 (March, 1973).

————. "Final Report on the Pyramid Lake Pilot Project, 1970–1975," mimeographed report prepared by the Laboratory of Atmospheric Physics (January, 1977).

————. Atmospheric Sciences Center. "1978–1980 State Weather Modification Program: Biennial Report."

————. President's Annual Report, 1977–78.

Wall Street Journal (August 10, 1979), 1: 1, 21: 1–3.

Washington Post (August 7, 1966): A–4; (August 28, 1966): L7.

Wier, Jeanne Elizabeth, sponsor. *Nevada: A Guide to the Silver State,* American Guide Series of the Works Project Administration (Portland: Binfords and Mort, 1940).

Wiley, Peter, and Robert Gottlieb. *Empires in the Sun: The Rise of the New American West* (New York: G. P. Putnam and Sons, 1982).

Wolfe, Tom. *The Kandy-Kolored Tangerine-Flake Streamline Baby* (New York: Farrar, Straus, and Giroux, 1965).

Zeh, Charles H. "Nevada's Response to Crime: Rethinking the Use of Incarceration," *Nevada Public Affairs Review: Social Problems—Nevada's Solutions,* No. 1 (Reno: University of Nevada Bureau of Governmental Research, 1980), pp. 32–38.

INDEX

Alamo, 118
Allen, Gracie, 20
American Mining Congress, 49
American Stock Exchange, 76
Anderson, Blaine (Judge), 34, 36
Arizona v. California, 38
Atlantic City, 67, 81
Austin, 6, 17; population 16

Baring, Walter S., 49
Basic Magnesium Plant, 21, 26, 37
Basin and Range, 48
Bastian, Cyril, 77, 102
"Battle-Born: MX in Nevada" (television documentary), 58
Battle Mountain, 6; population, 18
Bible, Alan, 30, 49
Blacks, population, 91–94
Boulder City, 20, 27–28
Boulder Dam. *See* Hoover Dam
Bowler, Alida, 95
Bradhurst, Stephen T., 58
Britain, gambling in, 83–84
Bulletin of the Atomic Scientists, 57
Bunkerville, 20, 118
Burford, Robert, 55
Burns, George, 20

Caesar's Palace, 77
Cahill, Robbins, 70f
Calhoun, John C., 4
Caliente, 6, 77, 102
California-Nevada Interstate Compact Commission, 35
Cannon, Howard, 59, 119
Carlin, 18
Carson City, population, 8, 13, 14, 42
Carson River, 5, 29, 35, 41–42, 45
Carson-Truckee region, 5, 11–15
Carson Valley, 3, 14
Carter, Jimmy, 55
Catholics, 90, 117, 118, 120
Chinese population, 99
churches, 117–120
City of Trembling Leaves, The, 11
Civil rights, 91–94
Clark County, 5, 6–7, 20, 24, 41, 57, 77, 98, 119. *See also* Las Vegas
Clark, Walter Van Tilburg, 11–12, 65–66
Clean Air Act, 54
Colliers, 88–89, 90, 101
Colorado River, 7, 20, 29, 30, 36–40
Community Colleges, 106
Comstock Lode. *See* Virginia City
Constitution, Nevada, 51–52, 104
Coyote Springs, 41, 57

Dann, Carrie, 57
Dawes Act (1887), 94
Del Webb Corporation, 78
De Quille, Dan, 1
Desert Challenge, 8–9, 32
Desert Inn, 77–78
Desert Land Act, 49
Desert Research Institute. *See* University of
  Nevada
Deutsch, Albert, 88–89, 90, 91, 101, 113
Devil's Hole, or "pupfish" lawsuit, 43
Draft Environmental Impact Statement
  (DEIS), 58–59

East Ely, 6
education, 77, 100–112
Eisenhower, Dwight D., 20
Elko, 6, 105, 112; population, 8, 18
Elliott, Russell, 2
El Rancho Vegas, 21
Ely, 2, 4, 6, 16, 17, 122; population, 8, 16
Emery, LaVerne, 62
Empires in the Sun, 119
Endangered Species Act, 54
Equal Rights Amendment (ERA), 99–100,
  119
Eureka, 6, 17, 122; population, 16

Fair Housing Law, 93
Fallon, 5, 31; population, 15, 33
Federal Land Policy and Management Act
  (FLPMA), 50–55
Federal Register, 62
Fernley, 5, 31, 33
Fields, W. C., 20
FLPMA. *See* Federal Land Policy and Man-
  agement Act
Ford Foundation, 95
Fradkin, Philip, 40, 53
Frémont, John, 3
Frenchman Valley, 60

gambling, 2, 11–12, 14, 21, 35, 65–86 pas-
  sim, 113–115
Gannett newspapers, 82
George Peabody College for Teachers, 101
Goldfield, 2, 4, 6, 17, 122; population, 16
Gold Hill, 15, 17
Gottlieb, Robert, 119
Graham, Billy, 117

Gray, W. Howard, 49
Greenspun, Hank, 71, 78

Hannifan, Philip, 79, 80
Harnar, Nellie, 97
Harold's Club, 14
Harper's, 100
Harrah, William, 78
Hartman, Leon, 106
Hawke, James P., 44
Hawthorne, 6; population, 15
Henderson, 20, 26–27
Hicks, Marion, 71–72
higher education, 101, 105–112
Hilton Hotels, 78
Hispanics, 98
Hoffa, Jimmy, 77
Hollywood, 20, 85
Homestead Act, 49
Hoover, J. Edgar, 76–77, 119
Hoover Dam, 7, 20, 26–28, 37–38, 45, 59,
  112
Hopkins, Sarah Winnemucca, 97
House of Cards, 83
Hughes, Howard, 21, 77–79, 113, 119
Humboldt region, 5–6, 13, 18–19, 42,
  53
Humboldt River, 41–42, 45

immigrants, 98–99
Indian Reorganization Act (1934), 94
Indians. *See* Native Americans

Jackass Flat, 60
Jenkins, Bruce, 61
Johnson, Edward, 97–98
Johnson, Lyndon, 93
Jones, Clifford, 69f

Kansas City, 81
Kefauver, Estes, 69f, 76
Knisley, Ray, 77

Lahontan, Lake, 29
Las Vegas, 6–7, 19–28, 118; population, 7–
  9, 20–23; water problems, 36–41; reputation, 85–86; university in, 107–112
Las Vegas Age, 19

Las Vegas Bombing and Gunnery Range, 49, 60
Las Vegas Paiute colony, 97
Las Vegas Perspectives, 24
Las Vegas Sun, 71, 78
Last Frontier, 21
Latter-day Saints, 3, 7, 36, 57, 79, 90, 100, 117–121
Lattin, Ralph, 73
Laxalt, Paul, 60, 76, 77–79, 108
Laxalt, Robert, 16, 80–81
Lewis, Oscar, 11
Lillard, Richard, 13, 32; quoted, 8–9
Lincoln, Abraham, 3, 95
List, Robert, 45, 59, 81–83, 85, 104, 105, 109–110
Logan (Logandale), 20, 118
Lovelock, 6, 122; population, 18
Lund, 118, 122

McCarran, Patrick, 69–70
McGill, 16
McPhee, John, 48
Marvel, John, 49
Mead, Lake, 26, 37–39
Merrill, Charles, 74
Mesquite (township), 20, 118
Metro-Goldwyn-Mayer (MGM), 78
Miller, Max, 11
Mina, 6
Minden-Gardnerville, 5
Mining booms, 1–2, 4
Mining zone, 6, 15–18
Moapa, 20, 118
Moore, William, 69
Morals Legislation without Morality, 120
Morgan, Dale, quoted, 13–14
Mormon Country, 117–118
Mormons, *See* Latter-day Saints
Morrill Act (1862), 105
MX. *See* U.S. Air Force

National Environmental Policy Act, 54
Native Americans, 94–98. *See also* names of individuals and tribes
Nevada Bureau of Mines, 106
Nevada Commission on Equal Rights of Citizens, 92–93
Nevada Department of Conservation and Natural Resources, 45

Nevada Division of Water Planning, 44, 45, 54
Nevada Historical Society, 67
Nevada Humanities Committee, 58
"Nevada Plan" for educational funding, 102f
Nevada Resort Association, 77
Nevada Tax Commission, 68f
Nevada Test Site (NTS), 60–64
New Catholic Encyclopedia, 117
Newlands, Francis G., 5
Newlands Reclamation Project, 5, 15, 31–34 passim
Newsweek, 24, 52
New York Stock Exchange, 79
New York Times, 75, 76
North Las Vegas, 19, 20, 24–26

O'Callaghan, Mike, 79, 84, 93, 103, 109
O'Farrell, Thomas, 62
Ogden, Peter S., 3
Oriental population, 99
Orr Ditch case, 32–34
Overton, 20

Pahranagat Valley, 39
Paiute Indians, 29, 32–36 passim
Panaca, 118
Peabody plan for educational reform, 101–102, 103
Pioche, 6, 14, 17, 27, 62–64, 122; population, 16
Pittman, Vail, 68, 71
Preston, 118
Prisons, 91
Proposition 6 (Nevada), 104
Proposition 13 (California), 104
Prostitution, 9
Pyramid Lake, 42, 45
Pyramid Lake Indian Reservation, 32, 94–96, 97

Railroads, 6, 17, 19–20, 48, 96
Railroad Valley, 39
Reagan, Ronald, 41, 44, 53, 55, 60, 85
Reno, 5, 14; population, 8–9, 14, 33; reputation, 11–13; university in, 105–112 passim; water problems, 32f, 44
Reno-Sparks Indian Colony, 94
Rhoads, Dean, 51
Roughing It, 65

Rudolph, Frederick, 105
Rusco, Elmer, 89–90, 92, 94
Russell, Charles, 70–73 passim, 101, 102
Rutgers University, 120
Rye Patch reservoir, 42

Sagebrush Alliance, 57f; proposed, 114–122
    passim
Sagebrush Casinos, 11
Sagebrush Rebellion, 50–55
Sampson, Dewey, 94–95
Santini, Jim, 59
Sawyer, Grant, 75–77, 108
S.B. 92, gambling control bill, 72–73
School Support Tax, 102
Shoshone Indians, 57, 95
Siegel, Benjamin "Bugsy," 21, 68
Sierra Club, 62
Sinatra, Frank, 85
Skolnick, Jerome, 83–84
Smith, Alfred Merritt, 30, 36, 44, 45
Smith, Jedediah, 3
Smith, Raymond I., 14
Smith Valley, 5
Southern Pacific Transportation Co., 96
Sparks, 5; population, 8, 14
Squires, Charles P., 19, 20, 32
Stegner, Wallace, 117–118
Stewart, Helen, 97
Stewart Indian School, 97
Stout, Minard W., 107–108

Tahoe, Lake, 14, 19, 32–36; population, 35
Tax Commission v. Hicks, 71–75
Taylor Grazing Act, 49
Teamsters' Union, 77
Te-Moak bands. *See* Shoshone
Thompson, Gordon, 93
Thunderbird Hotel case, 70–75
Tonopah, 2, 4, 6, 17; population, 16
Townley, John, 33
Truckee-Carson Irrigation District. *See* New-
    lands Reclamation Project
Truckee River, 5, 29, 32–36, 41, 42, 95
Turner, Stansfield, 57
Turner, Wallace, 75f
Twain, Mark, 1, 35, 65

Union of Concerned Scientists, 57
Union Pacific Railroad, 19

University of Nevada: Bureau of Gov-
    ernmental Research, 89; Desert Research
    Institute (DRI), 40–43, 78, 108; in Reno,
    31, 40, 78, 101, 105–112, 121; in Las
    Vegas, 107–112, 121
U.S. Air Force, MX missile proposal, 41,
    43–44, 55–60, 62, 95, 116, 119, 121
U.S. Army Corps of Engineers, 42
U.S. Atomic Energy Commission (AEC),
    60f
U.S. Bureau of Land Management (BLM),
    44, 50–55
U.S. Bureau of Reclamation, 27, 34
U.S. Central Intelligence Agency (CIA),
    57
U.S. Civil Aeronautics Board, 82
U.S. Department of Agriculture, 54
U.S. Department of the Interior, 54
U.S. District Court, 32–34
U.S. Federal Bureau of Investigation (FBI),
    76, 80, 81, 114, 119
U.S. Forest Service, 35
U.S. Geological Survey, 31
U.S. Internal Revenue Service (IRS), 80,
    114–115
U.S. Justice Department, Organized Crime
    Strike Force, 81
U.S. Ninth Circuit Court, 34
U.S. Public Land Law Review Commission,
    49–50
U.S. Securities and Exchange Commission,
    80
U.S. Supreme Court, 31, 34, 38

Vaughan, Robert, 72–73
Virginia City, 1, 5, 13, 15, 17, 65–66; pop-
    ulation, 16

Walker River, 29, 35, 41–43 passim
Walker River Indian Reservation, 42, 94,
    96, 97
Warburton, Joseph, 42
Washoe County, 36. *See also* Reno
Washoe Project, 42
Washo tribe, 94
Washington Post, 76
Watasheamu Reservoir (proposed), 42
Watt, James, 53, 55
Weber Reservoir, 42
Wells, 6

Wendover, 19
West, Mae, 20
Westside, Las Vegas, 19, 92
Wier, Jeanne, 67
Wiley, Peter, 119
Winnemucca, 6, 122; population, 8, 18
Winters Doctrine, 31–34 passim, 40, 96
Wolfe, Tom, 85–86, 87

Works Projects Administration (WPA) guide, 19, 67–68

Yerington, 5, 14
Young, Clifton, 52
Yucca Valley, 60

Zeh, Charles, 91